William Henry Giles Kingston

Antony Waymouth

Or The Gentlemen Adventurers

William Henry Giles Kingston

Antony Waymouth
Or The Gentlemen Adventurers

ISBN/EAN: 9783337177577

Printed in Europe, USA, Canada, Australia, Japan

Cover: Foto ©ninafisch / pixelio.de

More available books at **www.hansebooks.com**

ANTONY WAYMOUTH;

OR,

THE GENTLEMEN ADVENTURERS.

BY

WILLIAM H. G. KINGSTON.

BOSTON:
J. E. TILTON AND COMPANY.
1865.

STEREOTYPED BY
C. J. PETERS & SON,
No. 13 Washington St.

Press of Geo. C. Rand & Avery.

ANTONY WAYMOUTH.

CHAPTER I.

"What! Ned Raymond ahoy! Heave to, lad. What! dost seek to give a wide berth to an old friend? That once was not your wont. Ned Raymond ahoy, I say!"

The slight dark mustache on the lip of the person addressed showed that he had just reached the age of manhood. His raven hair hung in ringlets from his head. A black velvet cloak thrown over one shoulder, and a tightly-fitting dress of the same material and hue, set off his well-made, active figure. His plumed cap and the sword by his side showed that he claimed to belong to the upper rank of society. Indeed, no one looking at the refined expression of his features and his intelligent countenance could doubt that such was his right. He was walking somewhat rapidly through the narrow and irregularly-built streets of the seaport town of Plymouth, at that time one of the chief ports of departure for the numerous naval expeditions which went forth to the West and to the East in search of new lands, and of regions of gold and diamonds and other precious stones.

It is worthy of remark that the people of Devonshire and Cornwall have from the earliest days shown a strong propensity for naval adventure. This arises not alone from their geographical position, but has descended to them from their progenitors, who were, there can be but little doubt, Phœnicians, — or their descendants the Carthaginians, perhaps, — sailors, merchants, and others attracted from the northern shores of Africa for the sake of the tin found in those counties. Even at the present day many of their customs and the nautical terms they employed are retained. The clotted cream of Devonshire and on the coast of Barbary is the same, as is the mode in which the people manage their farms. Caboose was the name of the temple carried by the fire-worshipping Phœnicians on the decks of their vessels; the cook's house on board ship is now so called. Davit in Arabic is a crooked piece of wood; the same term we apply to the timbers by which boats are hoisted up to the sides of ships. However, we are now talking of more modern days, and must proceed.

Good Queen Bess sat on the throne of England, and ruled the realm as few sovereigns have done before or since, greatly to the furtherance of Britain's glory and wealth, and to the firm establishment of religion and true liberty, for which let all honest Englishmen be grateful, and talk not of her womanly weaknesses and failings.

The young gentleman, hearing his name called, stopped and looked earnestly at the person who had addressed him, and who was following rapidly in his footsteps. The costume of his pursuer was far more gay and dashing than was his, being composed of bright-colored velvet and silks, with a golden chain round his neck, a plumed hat set jauntily on his head, and a jewel-hilted sword by his side. He had a laughing blue eye and light curling locks, and though his countenance was well bronzed, and his voice strong and manly, his features still bore the impress of early youth. Indeed, his hairless lip and beardless chin showed that he had scarcely emerged from boyhood. He ran up to the person of whom he was in pursuit, and frankly held out his hand.

"Really, sir, you have the advantage of me," said the elder gallant, gravely drawing himself up.

On this the younger gave way to a merry peal of laughter, exclaiming, "If I am changed, surely you are not, good coz.' I see that. What! Ned — Ned, most oblivious of mortals, don't you remember little Tony Waymouth, whom you pulled out of the water just in time to prevent him from becoming food for the fishes, at the risk of your far more valuable life, and to whom you ever gave the best of advice, and set the best of examples, neither of which, graceless vagabond that he was, is, and I fear ever will be, he took or followed?"

There was no longer any hesitation on the part of the elder in seizing the proffered hand, but he found his fingers wrung in so hearty a way, and with so vice-like a grasp, that he could scarcely refrain from crying out with pain.

The lad saw by the expression of his friend's countenance that in the warmth of his affection he had really hurt him.

"Marry, pardon me, dear Ned, that my fingers have been thus heedless. They have been so accustomed to haul at ropes, tug at the oar, and dabble in the tar-bucket, that they have, like their owner, lost, I fear me, all civilized habits and customs," he exclaimed, exhibiting his horny-palmed, thoroughly-bronzed hand.

"Say not a word, Tony," answered Raymond. "Far rather would I feel the grasp of thy honest fist than the gingerly touch of the soft-palmed courtier. But tell me, lad, where hast thou been these long years since we parted at school, where I fear me, Tony, there was not much knowledge packed away in that then small head of thine? I have heard rumors of your existence, and that is all."

"Wandering over the ocean, and battling with the elements and strong-armed men," answered young Waymouth. "But the spectacle of two such gay gallants as we are in this quiet street has already attracted attention. I see down there the sign of the White Swan, a good hostelrie, I know. Let us step in there; it is about the hour of dinner, and I know full well that we shall find a cup of good sack to wash down the viands. While discussing it I will tell you briefly of my doings and listen gladly to yours. I long to hear of your past life and future prospects."

"Agreed," said Raymond; "but before we enter let me advise you, Tony, to take but one cup; the second is apt to do harm."

"An' it be a jolly big one, then," answered Waymouth, as they entered the inn. "We rovers of the sea get so much salt water down our throats that we require a fair portion of good liquor to correct its ill effects."

"The same as of old," observed Raymond, as they took their seats in the public room and waited till dinner was placed before them, preceded by the promised sack. "And now, Tony, that your throat is washed, tell me all that time will allow of yourself," he added, after Waymouth had tasted and expressed his approbation of the sack.

"With all my heart, then, that I may the sooner come at yours, Ned, I'll begin," said Waymouth, in his light, cheery tone. "You know that I always had a fancy for a life at sea; not that I knew any thing about it, but I thought I did, which comes to the same thing. Many of my relatives followed the sea, both on my father's and mother's side, and among them was as brave a gentleman as ever stepped — my worthy cousin, Captain John Foster, of the good ship Primrose, belonging to the port of London. I had frequently seen him and won his regards, and so at last I told him my hopes and wishes. He promised to intercede for me, and kept his word. My father gave his consent, and the next time he put to sea he took me with him as cabin-boy. The Primrose was bound for Bilboa, on the north coast of Spain, with bale goods. We had a quick run across the Bay of Biscay, were politely received by the Spaniards, and soon made arrangements to dispose of our cargo. To show his regard, the chief magistrate of the district, the corregidor, sent word that he would pay us a visit. He came off in a large boat, with a dozen or more dons, highly respectable merchants, he told us, who wished to make our acquaintance. The captain introduced me to the corregidor as a young relative who had come to sea for the first time to try how he liked a life on the ocean. The magistrate made a great deal of me, and patted me on the head, and said all sorts of complimentary things which I didn't understand; but there was a language in his eye which I did understand, though, and I saw glances exchanged between him and the dark eyes of his companions which still further aroused my suspicions. I slipped out of the cabin and told the captain. 'Good boy!' he remarked; 'I'm on the watch.'

"Dinner was brought in, and wine in abundance.

The corregidor, after sparingly partaking of some food and wine, departed with some of his followers, leaving, however, five in the cabin, who at once made themselves at home, laughing, and singing, and talking at their ease, trying to make the captain and officers drink with them. I observed that they did not swallow nearly as much as they pretended to take, and that the flasks but slowly became empty. They kept on their cloaks, and I caught sight of the scabbards of their swords and of a long dagger in the belt of one of them. Still we mustered twenty-seven men, stout and true, on board, so that we had nothing to fear from these five Spaniards. As to purchasing the cargo, the object for which they said that they had come, they were, it seemed, too much overcome with wine to talk about the matter.

"Leaving them in the cabin, I went on deck, where I found that the captain had served out arms to all the men, and loaded the guns ready for action. Some of our people were sent below, others lounged about the deck with their weapons concealed under their clothes. He had good reason for this precaution, for as I looked over the side I saw two boats pulling off towards us, one containing twenty or thirty men, the other near a hundred, it seemed.

"The corregidor, in the smaller boat, was the first to come alongside and to step on board with all imaginable frankness and cordiality. He had brought with him some dozen or more Biscayan merchants, who were desirous of trading with their friends the English.

"'If these are Biscayan merchants, they have a very martial look about them,' observed the captain to one of our officers. 'Now, Senhor Corregidor,' he continued, 'you'll understand that no more of those gentry come up the side; they crowd our decks and incommode the men in their duties.'

"The corregidor with many a grin agreed to this, but still the boats remained alongside. Our captain on this was about to order them off, when Senhor Corregidor whips out a white wand of office, and cries out in a loud voice, 'Yield, for you are our prisoners,' while the seeming merchants draw their daggers and swords and present them at the captain's breast.

"'We are betrayed, lads!' he shouts, knocking up the weapons with a handspike.

"At the same moment a drum beats in the big boat, and the Spaniards, soldiers in disguise, begin to climb up the sides. I run aft and clap the hatch over the cabin, so as to keep the five gentlemen there quiet, while our men, drawing out their weapons, begin to lay about them with a will which astonishes the dons. Some run to the guns and point them down at the boats; others, with axes, force back the men who are climbing the sides. Our decks are slippery with blood. Several of our men are wounded. A shot strikes a shipmate standing in front of me, and, falling dead, he knocks me over. It saves my life, for a Spaniard is making a cut at me, which misses, and our captain cuts him

down. Still we fight on against fearful odds. Our enemies gain the deck, but it is only to add to the heap of the slain. At last the corregidor cries out, and begs our captain to order his men to cease fighting.

"'Marry, very likely!' says the captain, in the sort of Spanish lingo he spoke. 'Why, my fellows are such fire-eating dogs that they would kill me if I was to make such a proposal. Is it the Inquisition, with a turn at the thumb-screws, the rack, and the stake, or liberty and Old England, you look for, my brave lads?' continues the captain, turning to the men.

"'Liberty and Old England!' shout all our company.

"'Then let us trundle these treacherous scoundrels overboard, cut our cable, and make sail,' he exclaims in return.

"Scarce a minute passed and it was done; some were thrown into the hold, and the rest overboard, and a strong breeze coming off the land, the cable was cut, the sails filled, and away we glided out ahead of a dozen boats which came off in pursuit. We plied them well with our ordnance, till, like baffled hounds, they turned tail and went back to their kennel.

"Clear of the land, we turned to examine our prisoners. The five caged in the cabin had whole skins, the rest were wounded. Among them was the smooth-spoken corregidor, now wofully crestfallen. We dressed his and the other people's hurts as well as we could, seeing that we had no leech aboard, and with a fair wind stood across the Bay of Biscay. The captain, whose kindness seemed to touch the feelings of the don, at last asked him what made him act so treacherous a part. On this out of his pocket he pulls a paper, which was just an order from King Philip to seize every ship of Holland, Zealand, Easterland, and England, in his ports, letting none escape, that he might increase his own fleet, by which he proposed to strike a blow to overwhelm Old England and all Protestant countries together.

"'Ah! is that so, Senhor Don? Then our gracious sovereign lady shall know all about it, an' my name be John Foster,' exclaimed the captain; and you may be sure that, favored by fine weather, we carried all sail night and day until we arrived safely in the Thames.

"The captain, taking me with him, hurried up to London with our prisoners, strongly guarded. We got audience of the queen and of the great Lord Burleigh; and the captain, albeit not much of a courtier, did his devoir right courteously to her majesty, who took the paper with her own gracious hand, and ordered a gentleman standing by to read it to her. When she heard its contents her whole countenance changed.

"'We'll be on the watch for you, cousin Philip,' she exclaimed; but I heard no more, for her majesty turned to my Lord Burleigh and other noblemen and gentlemen to hold secret converse with them.

"But the captain was not the man to go away without fulfilling all his intentions. He took me by the hand, and, presenting me to the queen, told her that I had given him the first hint of the intentions of the Spaniards, and confirmed the opinion he had formed, and he hoped that her majesty would graciously keep me in mind.

"'Ah, ah! the little varlet, we'll not forget him,' was her majesty's reply; nor, by my troth, did she. There's not an expedition of note, nor an adventure which has promised honor or wealth, since undertaken, in which I have not been engaged. I sailed with Admiral Sir Francis Drake to the West Indies in the Sea Dragon, commanded by honest Harry White. We did the Spaniards no small damage, burning their towns and sinking their ships without number, and came back with our pockets lined with doubloons, and six hundred thousand golden pounds, and brass cannon, and jewels, and ornaments of all sorts on board. I served aboard the Mary Rose, under the brave Captain Fenton, when the Spaniards' Grand Armada entered the Channel; and, following them up, we at length broke through their line, led by the admiral himself. Then we engaged broadside to broadside a huge Spanish galleon, which we compelled to strike, and carried into port. But I weary you, good coz, with my adventures; I might go on talking till midnight, and yet not tell thee half the things I have done and seen. I may well say, that, since the time I made my first voyage in the Primrose, for not one single month at a time has my foot rested on *terra firma*."

"Weary me, Tony!" exclaimed Raymond, who had been listening with the deepest attention, and an expression of wonder in his countenance, to every word his young companion had uttered. "Indeed you do not. If I did not know you to have been as a boy the soul of honor, and incapable of falsehood, I should only have been inclined to doubt that you had gone through all the adventures you describe."

"Ah, that is because all these years you have been living quietly on shore, as I suspect, where weeks and months pass by you scarcely know how," answered Waymouth, in a tone of compassion. "But now that I have told you somewhat about my worthless self, let me ask you how you have passed the last few years of your mortal existence?"

"Briefly I will reply," said Raymond. "At school and college. The learned University of Oxford is my *alma mater*, and even now I am debating to what profession to devote my energies — the law, the Church, or physic. Sometimes I fancy public life, or to seek my fortune at court, where I have kindred who might aid me; but yet, in truth, I am undecided."

"Ah, that's good," exclaimed Waymouth with animation. "The law — to persuade your hearers that black is white, and to set men by the ears — let that alone an' you value your soul."

It is not surprising that the young seaman should give expression to a vulgar and ignorant prejudice against one of the most necessary of professions.

"Physic! 'Throw physic to the dogs, I'll none on't,' as Will Shakspeare has it," continued Waymouth. "No, no, Ned, learn not to murder thy friends and those that trust thee. As to the Church, I'll say nothing against that if thou hast a calling to the ministry. To care for the soul's welfare is a noble office, but if sought for the sake of filthy lucre it's a mean, despicable trade, so we hold who follow the sea. And then thou talkest of seeking thy fortune at court. As well seek it on the slippery ice. No, no; listen to me, Ned. Seek it with us. It's a secret as yet, and I cannot tell thee particulars; but this much I may say. There is as bold an adventure even now preparing as ever set forth from these shores. Hark, Ned: I know that thou art trustworthy. It is for the far-off lands of India, Cathay, the Spice Islands, and maybe the wide Pacific, where many a richly laden galleon or Portugal ship may be fallen in with. Become an adventurer with us. Our lists are not filled up. Think that in two or three short years, at most, thou wilt become for certain a man of wealth, fit to wed the proudest lady in the land. Then the wonders of those distant lands! They make no more count of gold and silver, of diamonds and other precious stones, than we do of tin and iron, and of pebbles from the seaside. Come, come, Ned; say yes to my proposal."

But Raymond did not say yes, and Waymouth continued in the same strain for some considerable time longer. At length Raymond answered, while the color mantled on his cheeks—

"I would fain go with thee, good coz, but the truth is, there is one I love here in England from whom I could not bear to be parted. We trust to wed some day, and all my hopes of happiness on earth are bound up in her."

"Ha! ha! I might have thought so," said Waymouth. "That comes of living on shore. Now at sea we have no time for thinking of such matters. I doubt not, however, that the fair one, whoever she may be, is worthy of your love. Tell me, do I know her?"

"It is no secret—she is the Lady Beatrice Willoughby. Her grandfather was that noble captain who perished in the attempt to discover a passage to Cathay by the north-west. You have doubtless heard the tale—how he and all his men were found frozen to death in the icy sea, the admiral seated in his cabin, his pen in his hand, his journal before him."

"Ay, that have I, and reverence his name," said Waymouth with feeling. "But what fortune hast thou, coz, to support a wife? They say these ladies of fashion are not content unless they have their coach, their running footmen, and their waiting-women, and I know not what else beside."

Raymond sighed. "My fortune is to be made—I live on hope," he answered.

"Such often maketh the heart sick and the body lean," replied the young sailor. "Follow my advice. Go tell the Lady Beatrice the truth. Vow eternal constancy, and comfort her with all the soothing speeches thou canst make, and I'll warrant that, in three short years at furthest, thou wilt return with wealth sufficient to support a wife as becomes your family and hers."

There can be no doubt that Antony Waymouth spoke what he believed to be the truth, and gave, as he fancied, excellent advice. It may appear surprising, however, that Raymond, a scholar and a man of good parts and judgment, should have been so strongly influenced as he was by the arguments of a mere youth; but, as far as acquaintance with the world was concerned, Waymouth was the oldest of the two. He had been left since a child almost to work his own way in the world, helped onward by the queen, and had mixed with every variety of men. This gave him a confidence in himself and an independence of manner which Raymond had had no opportunity of gaining.

While the young men were still eagerly talking, a clock from a neighboring tower struck the hour of one past noon. Waymouth started up with an exclamation of astonishment, saying —

"The hours have sped faster than I thought. I should have been aboard by this time to see how the artificers get on with their fittings. But come, coz, you shall be my excuse, and I'll show thee as stout ships as ever sailed the salt ocean."

"Agreed," was the answer, and the two friends set off. All the way Antony plied his companion with the most glowing descriptions of the wealth and fortune to be obtained in the distant East, not to speak of the honor, and glory, and renown. Portugal ships and Spaniards without number were sure to be taken, even should the land fail to yield what might be expected. And then the wonders to be seen — the curious people — the palaces of silver and precious stones — the Great Mogul on his throne of gold, and the Emperor of Cathay, with his robes of rubies and diamonds — not to speak of the possibility of falling in with Prester John, whose dominions were undoubtedly on that side of Africa; and then the Spice Islands, which might be discerned by their fragrance even when miles away!

Enlarging, as Waymouth did, with an eloquence which perfect confidence in the truth of what he was saying gave him, and a strong desire to gain over his friend, it is not surprising that Raymond yielded to such seductive arguments, and began to grow eager to join the expedition as an adventurer. Aboard the ships which were fitting in the harbor, Waymouth introduced him to several other adventurers, who naturally wished to obtain a gentleman of such good parts and family as a brother in their company. Raymond had, he fancied, a small patrimony at his command. Could he do better than risk it in so promising an adventure, and in three short years come back and marry his beloved Beatrice? Still he would do nothing rashly; he would make no engagement till he had talked the matter over with her. Accordingly, leaving Waymouth on board to attend to his nautical duties, early next morning he took horse and set off for Exeter, in the neighborhood of which city the Lady Willoughby, with her daughter and the rest of her family, resided.

Raymond was welcomed as he always was, but he could not bring himself at first to announce the object of his visit. He spoke, however, of his meeting with Waymouth, and of his descriptions of the wonders of the East, and the wealth to be speedily obtained in those distant seas. His auditors were even more interested than he expected. It was but natural that young Hugh Willoughby should be so, but so likewise was Hugh's uncle, Sir John Jourdan, a brother of Lady Willoughby's, and guardian to her children.

The early dinner over, Raymond and Beatrice wandered forth into the grounds, for they were acknowledged lovers, and enjoyed a liberty which would otherwise have been denied them. Raymond saw at once that Beatrice was sad at heart. He felt tongue-tied. She spoke first.

"I know what has been passing in your mind, dear Edward. You long to join these adventurers, and I know why — for the sake of the wealth you hope to obtain."

She gazed tenderly at him, her blue eyes suffused

with tears. Beatrice was fair and graceful. Raymond thought her beauty faultless: so did many others. How could he withstand such an appeal? He acknowledged that she was right in her conjectures, but expressed himself ready to be guided by her decision.

"Stay, then," she whispered. "Wealth I do not value. I would be content to be your wife however humble your lot, but I have that confidence in your steadiness, and perseverance, and love for me, that, with the many honorable careers open to you at home, I feel sure that you will ere long secure a sufficient competency to support me in that station of life in which we have been born."

Raymond thanked her over and over again for this kind and encouraging speech. In a moment all his dreams of adventure and the wealth he was suddenly to acquire vanished into thin air. He promised to be worthy of the high opinion she had formed of him, and to labor on bravely in England, having the enjoyment and support of her society. They wandered on through the grounds, beneath the shade of stately elms and sturdy oaks, in the delightful feeling that they were not to be parted, and regardless of all sublunary affairs but their own. Little, therefore, were they prepared for the blow which was to fall on their heads on their return to the hall in the evening.

It appeared as if both Sir John and Hugh had divined Raymond's thoughts when he had arrived in the morning at the hall, for they immediately commenced the subject of an adventure to Cathay, and inquired if he had formed any plans for making one. Raymond did not like the tone in which he was addressed, and replied simply that, had such an intention crossed his mind, he had abandoned it. On this the knight looked glum, and Hugh showed an inclination to fume; but no further words then passed.

It was not till the ladies had retired to their chambers that Sir John again opened on the subject. He spoke very explicitly. He was the guardian of his niece Beatrice, and as such had the undoubted disposal of her hand. Love and poverty might do in theory, but were objectionable in practice. He had a great respect for Master Raymond, as he had for Sir Thomas his father, and for all his family, but the interests of his ward must be his first consideration. Now he had discovered, *imprimis*, that Master Raymond had much less fortune than he had supposed; and, secondly, that his prospects of making a fortune, or of pushing his way in the world, were much smaller than desirable, and that, therefore, he was in duty bound to withhold the consent previously given to his marriage to Beatrice till such times as he could show that he possessed the means in fact, and not only in prospect, of maintaining her as a gentlewoman.

Poor Raymond felt his heart sinking lower and lower while listening to these remarks, till it seemed to have gone out of his bosom altogether. What could he say? He stammered out, at length, that his love would give him strength and courage to achieve any thing mortal man could do, and that he was sure of success. But what sounded a very plausible argument to his ears was so much prunella to those of the old knight.

"I'll tell thee what, lad: from thine own showing this morning, there is a course open to thee by which thou mayst gain speedily both wealth and honor, and all a gentleman of spirit can desire, and that I take thee to be. Go, think about it on thy couch, and to-morrow I'll warrant that thou wilt agree that I have given thee sound counsel and advice."

Edward went to his couch, but not a wink did he sleep. His heart was torn with a variety of conflicting emotions. He could not help owning that there was truth in what Sir John had said, and yet he felt that he had the power to win his way to fortune by honest labor with such a being as Beatrice Willoughby at his side. Hot and feverish, he rose early to take a turn in the park. He had not gone far when he heard footsteps behind him. He turned, and saw Hugh Willoughby following him at a rapid pace. There was a frown on the young man's brow, and his lips were compressed in a way which showed that he was in no good humor.

"Well met, this fine morning," he exclaimed in an angry tone. "I must have a word or two with you, Master Edward Raymond. It seems, sir, that you have been deceiving us — leading us to suppose that your fortune is far greater than it turns out to be. I'll tell you, sir, that my sister shall never wed a beggar while I have a sword with which to run that beggar through the body who dares to wish it." Edward gasped for breath — such bitter, taunting, cruel words, how could he abide them? He had a sword by his side, but nothing should make him draw it on the brother of his Beatrice. He took two or three turns up and down on the greensward.

"Hugh," he exclaimed, "you wrong me cruelly. Your uncle knows more of the state of my affairs than I do myself. My earnest desire has been to obtain a fortune to support your sister as becomes her. But two days ago the offer was made me to undertake such an expedition as that proposed by your uncle. Not your taunts, not your threats, not your anger, shall compel me to go; but I believe that I shall be doing right in going. On one condition I will consent — that no force or restraint be put on your sister's inclinations. If she cares no longer for me, let her marry whom she will; but if she remains faithful to me — as I know right well she will, and as I shall to her — then I have your word, that, on my return with the wealth I may have won, I may claim her as my bride."

"Fairly and right nobly spoken," exclaimed Hugh, who, though hot-tempered, was of a generous disposition, and had been worked up to act as he had done by his uncle. "Agreed — agreed; I'll tell Beatrice what you have said, and, no doubt, she will see its wisdom."

In more friendly intercourse than from their first meeting might have been expected, the two young men continued their walk, and returned to such a breakfast as is seldom, in these degenerate days, seen on the table.

Sorely against her judgment and inclination, Beatrice yielded to her uncle's demands. Deep was her sorrow at parting from Edward, and reiterated were their mutual vows of constancy; not that either had the slightest doubt of each other's devoted love. It was more for the sake of influencing others than themselves that vows were exchanged — that they might say, "We have vowed; we cannot break our vows."

Edward had to return home to make his preparations. The old knight, his father, heard of this his sudden resolve with a sorrowing heart. His own health had given way sadly of late. He knew that the change which no mortal can avoid must soon come upon him, and should his well-loved son go away, even for a few years, he could scarcely hope that his eyes would rest on him again on this side the grave. He was fully aware, too, of the perils, great and innumerable, to which he must inevitably be exposed. Still, though gentle and loving, he was stout of heart; peril had never daunted him.

If his son desired to go on this adventure, he would not withhold his consent. Lady Raymond was no more; but there was another member of his family, to part from whom cost Edward a severe pang — his lovely sister Constance. She was not only lovely, graceful, and good, but full of animation and spirit, combined with a calm courage and determination which, when difficulties came in her way, made her take pleasure in overcoming them. Few who observed her gentle and quiet demeanor would have supposed her likely to perform the deeds of devotion and courage of which she was capable.

"I wish that I were a man, that I, too, might take part in so gallant an enterprise, and win for myself such a bride as is your Beatrice," she exclaimed when her brother told her of his purpose; but she added, "and yet, dear Edward, it grieves me sorely to part with you. I would go myself, and yet I would not have you go; and yet, again, I cannot say you nay. Go, go! It must be so, I see, and I will join my prayers with those I know your sweet Beatrice will offer up night and day for your safe return."

"The die is cast," said Edward with a sigh, and he wrote to Waymouth to say he would join him. In the course of four days he set forth from Exeter, with a couple of packhorses to carry his worldly goods, and a serving-man, equipped for his projected voyage to the far East.

CHAPTER II.

A GOODLY fleet of stout ships, with bulging sails, and gayly-colored banners and streamers flying, sailed down Plymouth Sound before a favoring breeze, which promised to waft them along steadily towards the sunny latitudes of the tropics. There sailed the Red Dragon, of full three hundred tons and forty pieces of ordnance — the admiral's ship; and there was the Serpent, of not less than two hundred and fifty tons — the vice-admiral's ship; and the Lion, of not much less tonnage and armament than the Serpent; there was the Lion's Whelp, a tall ship, and two pinnaces, the Sunshine and Moonshine, the larger ships carrying each from one hundred to one hundred and thirty men, and the pinnaces thirty men each; and as for arms, besides great guns, they were amply provided with culverins, sakers, falconets, and murtherers, the latter unpleasantly-named pieces being similar to blunderbusses on swivels, and loaded with small shot, and scraps of iron, lead, or stones. No little squadron in those days could have been more amply equipped, provisioned, and found in every way, or better manned or commanded.

It must be remarked that the pictorial representations of ships of those days give us a very erroneous notion of what ships really were. Ships capable of performing long voyages in tempestuous seas, and ships on tapestry — worked by fair fingers, which, however ably they might have plied their needles, were scarcely capable of delineating accurately those wonderful constructions on which the eyes of the workers had probably never rested — are very different from each other. The ships now described sailing down Plymouth Sound were strongly-built craft, with bows not over-bluff and sides not over-high. They had erections on deck, both at the bows and stern, rising some five feet above it, or a little more, perhaps, on the top of which men could stand for fighting or working some of the sheets and braces of the lighter sails, while the halyards and other chief ropes lead to the main deck. In these said erections, or castles, as they were called, still to be seen in most foreign and many English merchantmen, somewhat modified and in more pacific guise, there were port-holes, with guns projecting from them both at the sides and outer ends, and also along the deck. Thus an enemy having gained the deck would be exposed to a hot fire from the defenders under shelter of the wooden walls of the two castles. On the fore and main mast the sails were square, and there were also staysails fore and aft. On the mizzen-mast there was a large lateen yard and sail, such as is still seen in the Mediterranean. It was a useful and powerful sail for plying to windward, gaff-sails not having then been invented. The tops were circular, and heavier than would now be approved of, but certainly not the heavy constructions they are represented in pictures. The holds of those vessels were very capacious, and the cabins were fitted not without regard to comfort and luxury, and were often richly ornamented.

Such was the squadron to which the Lion belonged, and on board the Lion sailed Antony Waymouth as master's mate or chief officer under the captain, and his friend Edward Raymond, to whom was awarded the office of cosmographer, he being at the same time an adventurer of some three hundred pounds. Of the Lion an honorable gentleman, John Wood, was captain, and Master James Walker, a truly worthy man, and pious withal, the minister. Captain Lancaster, a man of renown and valor, was the admiral and general; and Nicholas Parker, captain of the Serpent, the vice-admiral. Of the rest of the officers and gentlemen adventurers it is not necessary here to speak. That they were not a godless or a lawless company, intent only on plunder, may be proved by the following rules and articles set down for their guidance: —

"The usual service appointed by the Church of England to be said twice a day. Due reverence to be given to the ministers. Not to suffer swearing, dicing, card-playing, or other vain talk. Conspiring against the life of the general or any other in authority to be punished by death. To follow the admiral day and night, and no man to be so bold as to go before him. To speak with him every morning and night. Not to be more than an English mile from him. Signals: Not to give chase without the admiral's orders. Watchwords: 'If God be with us;' answer, 'Who shall be against us?' If an enemy be encountered, rather to be on the defensive than the offensive."

Waymouth showed these articles to Raymond, observing — "You see, Ned, we seamen are not the godless reprobates some who grow rich upon our toil and danger would wish to make it appear. Where would you find a more humble Christian man than good Master Walker, our minister? and surely the example he and the other chaplains of the fleet set is not without its due influence among the crews."

Waymouth spoke the truth. It was not till many years after this that the character of the British seaman changed very much for the worse. No chaplains were then sent to sea; religion was ignored, and, as a consequence, the mass of seamen became godless, swearing, vicious reprobates, little better than heathens in their religion or morality. On board Captain Lancaster's fleet, however, order was well maintained, and the ministers setting a good example, religion flourished more than among most communities on shore.

All honor be to our sea-going ancestors! They were brave, sincere, zealous, and energetic men;

black was black with them, and white white. They had, it must be owned, some queer notions as to right and wrong, and honest traders on the north of the line seemed to consider themselves justified in acting the part of pirates to the south of it. Like the Arabs of the desert, their hand was against every man, and every man's hand against them. In the East, Spaniards, Portugals, Hollanders, and English were at ceaseless war with each other; or when the Hollanders pretended to side with the latter, it was simply for the purpose of betraying them and injuring their commerce in those parts.

As Raymond stood on the aftercastle of the Lion, watching the fast-receding shores of Old England, his spirit sank within him. He was thinking — and shame to him if he was not — of Beatrice. Not for a moment did he doubt her love and constancy; but he thought of the dangers to which she might be exposed should troublous times again arise — of her grief should he not be destined to return. He had others, also, whom he loved at home; his widowed mother, his brothers, and, above all, his sister Constance, the dear friend of his Beatrice, unlike her in appearance, for Constance was a dark-eyed, dark-haired beauty, full of life and animation, but like her in goodness and sense, and the sweetness of her disposition. Hugh Willoughby affected her, but it was evidently with a mere boyish admiration, and she regarded him in no other light than as her friend's brother.

Edward's reveries were broken in on by Waymouth, who sprang up on the deck of the aftercastle and clapped him, as was his wont, on the shoulder, exclaiming —

"What! disconsolate, Ned? Turn thee about, lad; the old country will not move till we come back, depend on that. Look ahead! that's the way we seamen set our eyes. Even now the admiral has made a signal that several sail are in sight under all canvas, steering for the south. Spaniards or Portugals I hope they may prove, and if so, and we come up with them, thou'lt have the satisfaction of enjoying a sea fight before we've been forty-eight hours on the salt ocean."

Edward's attention was instantly aroused. Nothing in the then state of his feelings he would so much enjoy as a battle. Not that he had seen one, nor had he pictured its horrors very clearly to himself. Had he, possibly he would not have been so anxious for it. The hope of booty animated the ship's company generally, though some declared that it was the desire to destroy Papists, the born enemies of England, at which their minister, Master Walker, severely rebuked them, telling them that it was filthy lucre, and that alone, they desired, and that the sword was not the weapon to win men over to the truth, or to use against men who held not the truth.

"The sword repelleth friends," he continued. "Kind words and gentle usage attract those who have been our foes. Such are the weapons Protestants should use against their Papist adversaries."

Master Walker's plain speaking and honest dealing with those over whose spiritual welfare he had the charge made him generally beloved, though a few bad tempers disliked him. To Waymouth and Raymond he was a sincere and warm friend, as he was in truth, as far as they would let him, to all who sailed on board the fleet. The chase continued; but the strangers, whatever their nation, were fleet craft. So far they had been gained on as to be seen from the tops of the Lion. Though outnumbering the English, they continued their flight; southward they sailed, and southward after them sailed their pursuers. The Spaniards had received so many severe lessons of late that they had learned to consider discretion the best part of valor. Henceforth their history was to show a retrogressive movement. Their black injustice and horrible cruelties to the natives of Mexico and Peru were to meet with just retribution. The cries of thousands ascending from their inquisitorial prisons were not unheard. National sins were to meet with national punishment. They had been tried in the balance, and found wanting. So it has gone on. The land of Spain, bountifully blessed by Nature, still holds a people grovelling in the dust of ignorance and superstition. At that time it is difficult to overstate, though not to believe, the utter detestation in which the Spaniards were held by all true-hearted Englishmen, and in which the Portugals over whom they held sway had to share. The chase continued till night hid the strangers from the sharp eyes of the men on the lookout at the mast-heads. In vain were they looked for the next morning.

"Never mind," said Waymouth as he walked the deck; "the world is round: Sir Francis Drake has proved it so. We'll come up with them in the course of the circle."

The belief that the enemy were ahead urged the bold mariners to carry sail night and day, so that their run to the south was unusually rapid. Raymond devoted himself to the study of navigation and to practising the use of such nautical instruments as were then invented; nor did he neglect to gain a knowledge of the object of the ropes and sails, and the mode of dealing with a ship under various circumstances, so that Waymouth soon pronounced him an accomplished seaman. There occurred but one event worth narrating for some time. Sixteen sail were seen approaching, and the fleet got ready for action. The strangers, however, turned out to be Hamburg hulks from Lisbon; but the obstinate Hollanders refused to strike to the English flag — a piece of folly not to be borne — so they were fired into and compelled to heave to. Boats were then sent on board, and such articles as were likely to prove useful were taken out of them, it being evident that they were loaded with Spanish property. They were then charitably allowed to proceed on their voyage. We will not describe the mummeries and other ceremonies which took place on crossing the line, introduced by some Genoese seamen on board, such as they said their countrymen were wont to indulge in formerly on passing through the " Gut of Gibbelterra," and now of late in these same latitudes. It was not much to good Master Walker's taste, seeing that numerous profane gods and goddesses of the sea were introduced — Hercules and Orion, and Venus and Neptune, and others, Tritons and odd fish of all sorts. Without misadventure the squadron reached Sierra Leone, where the blacks were friendly, and, taking in water and fresh provisions, stood across to the coast of Brazil. Here a brighter lookout than ever was kept, and not without avail, for when about eight leagues from the shore they descried a small Portugal ship, which they chased and took, of about fifty tons' burden, bound up the River Plate. She had forty-two negroes on board for Peru, and two Portugal women and a child passengers, with some sugar, rice, and sweetmeats. The next day another Portugal ship was captured. Waymouth in his journal remarked, " that the only riches in her besides slaves and friars were beads, pictures, and other spiritual trinkets — furniture designed for the use of a new monastery."

The pilot of this ship turned out to be an Englishman — one Dick Carter, from Limehouse — who had been so long away from home that he had almost lost all use of his native tongue.

"Why, lad, we have a man aboard—Tom Carter—from the same place," observed Waymouth, as the man tried in broken accents to narrate his history.

Tom was sent for, and, sure enough, the two proved to be brothers. Dick gladly consented to serve on board the Lion, and informed Waymouth, in gratitude for his kind treatment, that a Spanish squadron of considerable force was daily expected in the Plate. The admiral, however, instead of trying to avoid them, resolved to await their coming, and, entering the river, cast anchor.

"Now, Ned, we shall have our hearts' desire," exclaimed Waymouth, as he stopped for a minute near his friend while going round the decks to see that the ship was ready for a fight.

The day was passing away, when, about four o'clock in the afternoon, five sail of large ships and several smaller ones were seen rounding a point in the river. The English, therefore, in warlike manner set their watch, the trumpets sounded, the drums beat, and the admiral opened fire on the approaching enemy, who, however, anchored out of shot, the better to prepare for the expected fight. They were some little time in doing this, and then once more they advanced, it being now nightfall. The wind had dropped, so the Spaniards' boats towed on their big ships with the intent of boarding the English. Both sides were, meantime, plying their guns and small arms with vigor; the

English with the greater success, as their men were more at liberty. The Spanish vice-admiral was seen with two smaller ships bearing down on the Lion; Captain Wood was, therefore, compelled to slip his cable, to prevent them driving athwart his hawse. A breeze springing up, he was able to make sail and lay the galleon alongside, caring little for the smaller ships. Now began a most desperate fight, the bright flashes of the guns making night appear like day; the rattle of the small arms, the roar of the heavy ordnance, the sounding of the trumpets and drums, the shouts and shrieks of combatants, creating a turmoil terrible to novices and confusing to the senses.

The Lion enjoyed a large share of the fight, everybody being actively engaged, the captain himself firing a musket like the rest. One of the Spanish frigates, coming too near her, received so heavy a storm of shot, that, one penetrating her magazine, with a loud roar she blew up, when her companion sheered off, not wishing to share the same fate. The Lion now turned her whole fury on the galleon, which she kept at a respectful distance. Suddenly the galleon's fire ceased. The darkness was great; she could nowhere be seen. Captain Wood now stood away to support the admiral and the other ships; they were hard pressed, though fighting valiantly. The Lion soon had an enemy worthy to contend with in a Portugal galleon which had come in with the Spaniards, and now hoped, by attacking a ship partly disabled by a long combat, to come off the conqueror. The English captain, as did his young lieutenant, called on their men to exert themselves to the utmost to fight for the honor of Old England. Raymond supported them bravely, and, though at length wounded in the arm, he refused to leave the deck. Thus the fight continued, Captain Wood making several attempts to board his opponent, which the latter nimbly avoided. The admiral and vice-admiral were all the time hotly engaged. The former was seen to run a large Spaniard aboard, when, after a hot discharge of great guns, flames were observed to burst forth from one ship or the other, and thus they drove by till no longer to be distinguished. The last seen of the Serpent was in chase of some Spaniard, as her tall masts, like some huge monster of the deep, glided by past the Lion. Towards morning the moon disappeared, clouds overspread the sky, the Portugal thought it wise to sheer off, and the brave ship's company of the Lion waited anxiously for daylight to ascertain the fate of their friends and foes. For fear of the ship being drifted on shore, Captain Wood again anchored.

As soon as the fight was over, Waymouth hastened to look for his friend. He found him below in the hands of the surgeon. Raymond bore the pain bravely. Waymouth congratulated him.

"You've had a taste of what a sea fight is like, Ned," he observed. "Maybe before we get back to Old England we may have to count scores such, for, no doubt, the Portugals and Spaniards, and even the Hollanders, will give us plenty of occasions to prove our valor."

Raymond replied that he was ready for another fight, and should be willing to meet the foes of England wherever they were to be found.

It appeared probable that he would at once have another opportunity, for, as daylight broke, a large ship was discerned bearing down on them under all sail. She was the Portugal. The Lion's crew flew to their guns, and as she came near plied her so well with their shot that she was fain to sheer off, and to stand down towards the river's mouth. As she stood away, an officer of rank — so he seemed by his fine garments and feather in his cap — sprang on the aftercastle, and, shaking his fist, cried out through his trumpet —

"We shall meet you again ere long, you hated English, and then we shall have our revenge."

"Let the dog bark who runs away. Though he shows his teeth he dare not use them," exclaimed Waymouth with a scornful laugh.

The increasing light had shown some way astern the topmasts of a ship out of the water, crowded with people. Was the foundered ship a friend or foe? As soon as they were clear of the Portugal ship two boats were lowered, and made towards the spot where the masts appeared. At the same time several boats were seen putting off from the shore,

clearly belonging to Spaniards. When they, on their part, beheld the English approaching, fearing their prowess, from which they had suffered so much, they put back, leaving their countrymen to their fate.

The poor people on the masts, who had been clinging there for the greater part of the night, held out their hands, imploring succor. This English sailors have ever been ready to give to those in distress, whether friends or foes. The boats, therefore, approached to take off the nearly-exhausted people. Waymouth, who was in the first boat, perceived, as he fancied, the flutter of a female's dress. On the cross-trees, just above the water, lay a young lady, her head resting on the arm of an old and dignified-looking man, while the two were further supported by four or five faithful seamen who clung near them. The seamen waved their hands to attract the notice of the English.

"Take this lady off first," they cried out. "Save her and her father; mind not us."

Waymouth required no further inducement to exertion than the sight that feminine gear had excited. The Spanish seamen refrained from leaping into the boat as she came up to the mast, allowing Waymouth to climb up and release the lady from her painful and perilous position. Carefully he lifted her into the boat, and placed her in the after-part.

"Oh, meu pai! meu pai!" she cried out in the

tongue of the Portugals—"Oh, my father! my father!"

"Have no fear, fair lady," cried Waymouth, who understood it slightly; "he is safe." And, springing back, he assisted the old gentleman into the boat. The latter, as far as his exhausted state would allow, expressed his thanks.

Not till now did the Spanish seamen descend into the boat. As soon as he had received as many as she could carry, Waymouth returned with them to the Lion. The care of the surgeon and good Master Walker soon restored the young lady—for young she was and beautiful—to a state of consciousness and quietude. Her nerves had been sorely shaken by the combat, the sinking of the ship, and terrible danger to which she had been exposed. Her father, the old gentleman, was, it appeared, Dom Joao Pinto d'Almeida, the governor of a Portugal settlement in the East; she was the Donna Isabel d'Almeida, his only child. Though Portugals, they had taken passage aboard this Spanish ship, intending to proceed on their farther voyage in the one which had escaped and left them to their fate. The Portugal ship was the Santa Barba, and her captain Dom Pedro de Lima. Dom Joao seemed glad to hear that the Santa Barba had escaped capture, and supposed that in the darkness Dom Pedro had not seen the wreck. Meantime most of the people from the masts had been rescued and brought on board the Lion.

While the boats were thus engaged, firing was heard, and several ships were seen approaching, hotly engaged, down the mighty Plate stream, compared to which the rivers of Europe seem but purling brooks. It was a sad fate for the poor wretches on the masts to be thus left to starve or fall off and be drowned, but there was no time for delay. The Lion lifted her anchor, and made sail to join in the combat. Her rigging had been repaired as far as practicable, so that she was fresh for the fight. The rest of the English squadron and four Spaniards or Portugals were observed fiercely exchanging shots with each other. The enemy, probably, had already enjoyed a sufficient taste of the quality of the English to be tired of the fight, for no sooner was the Lion observed drawing near with drums beating, trumpets braying forth defiance, and ordnance speaking a still more decided language, than they steered for the shore on either side, and ran hard and fast aground. Some of the people in the enemy's ships took to their boats, others leaped overboard and swam to the shore, and several were seen running backwards and forwards at their wits' end, the English cannon thundering furiously at them; while a few bold spirits stood at their quarters, and returned the fire from their own pieces. However, they could not long maintain the unequal fight; flames burst forth from the ports of the ships, and one after the other, before any booty could be obtained from them, they blew up, till not a Spaniard remained to dispute the passage of the river. Now the English admiral thought fit to anchor his fleet opposite a pleasant spot near the mouth of the river, and, the larger number of the company landing, a fort was erected to guard against surprise, and the repairing of the ships commenced.

As yet they had gained much of what men call glory and renown, concerning the value of which there may be some dispute; but they had obtained no booty, about the desirableness of which there cannot be two opinions. So thought the adventurers. They were all eager, therefore, to proceed to the East, where they expected to find it in abundance, and accordingly hurried on the refitting of the ships. It was well that they did so, for scarcely was the squadron once more clear of the land than a large fleet was seen approaching the mouth of the river. The English ships stood on their course, for the strangers, undoubtedly Spaniards and Portugals, were too numerous to be trifled with. The enemy were soon seen to make sail in chase. The English set all their canvas, not to avoid the fight, but to separate the ships of the enemy, so as to deal first with the faster sailers. The plan answered; but the leading Spanish ships soon got such a taste of the guns of the Dragon, the Serpent, and the Lion, that they dropped astern, the rest not deeming it prudent to take their places, content with boasting that they had put an English squadron to flight.

Thus triumphantly the English ships sailed on

their way across the Atlantic till they neared the Cape Bona Spei, or Bona Speranza, as in those days the Cape of Good Hope was frequently called. Once more they dropped anchor in Saldanha Bay, a place at which most vessels sailing to Cathay were wont to touch. The common people among the prisoners had been left on shore in America; but the officers and the Portugal governor and his daughter, and some attendants, had been carried on, the admiral deeming that they might be useful to exchange with any English persons of quality who might have been captured by the Portugals; or, if not, that a good ransom might be obtained for them. Dom Joao and Donna Isabel remained accordingly on board the Lion, where Captain Wood, as did his young lieutenant, paid them all the attention in their power.

Waymouth admired the fair captive. He could speak her language better than most on board, and many an hour, not unnaturally, he passed in her company. It is possible that his feelings might have run away with him altogether had he not had so grave a monitor as Edward Raymond by his side, who was ever whispering that Donna Isabel was of a country at enmity with his, of a faith differing greatly from his, and that, though her attractions were great, there were many fair ladies in England possessed of still greater, and more suited to be his bride. These remarks did not exactly go in at one ear and out the other; but no sooner did Donna

Isabel appear on deck than they were forgotten for the time. That Donna Isabel had, however, any other feeling than that of gratitude for Antony Waymouth, no one on board could say, for she was equally courteous to Raymond and to all the other officers.

Dom Joao meantime was very anxious to be liberated, as he wanted to get to his government, and he was continually urging his captors to allow him to depart on board the first Portugal ship they might meet, he undertaking to pay a large ransom for himself and daughter. Captain Wood was a jovial-hearted and mannered man. He laughed loudly at the proposal.

"Thine own ransom, worthy senhor, we shall fix at not less than five hundred golden pieces; and for thy daughter, we must allow Antony Waymouth to arrange that."

The captain spoke in jest, but to Waymouth the proposal caused sore perplexity. He was grieved to have to part with her, in the first place. In the second, if he named a ransom at what he considered her value, it would be high indeed; if he mentioned a small sum, it would appear as if he held her in low esteem. He was very much inclined to quarrel with his captain on the matter; but the more perplexed he appeared the more determined Captain Wood became to fix him to the point. He walked the deck in a state of great agitation. All sorts of mad schemes occurred to him.

He had paced up and down for some time when he was joined by Raymond, who had heard of his perplexity.

"Let me judge if I may help to get thee free of thy difficulty," said Raymond, who, having an older head on his shoulders, was not so troubled as his younger friend about the matter. "You have to name the value of this fair Portugal donna; you esteem her very highly too."

"Yes, indeed I do. She is the most charming, sweet, enchanting creature my eyes have ever beheld or expect to behold," exclaimed Waymouth, uttering many other rhapsodical expressions, which his friend did not interrupt. When he ceased, the latter quietly remarked —

"Well, repeat all you have said to our captain, and then declare that, as she is above all price, so no price would pay her ransom, and that, therefore, she is entitled to go free."

Waymouth struck his forehead, surprised that so bright a thought had never occurred to him, and, thanking Edward, hastened to the captain to give his reply.

It was taken in good part; no one was inclined to gainsay it; and Dom Joao undertook to pay the required sum, how, when, and where it might be demanded.

"At your own castle, when we can get there, and to whomsoever we may depute," was the reply.

Perfect confidence was placed in Dom Joao that

he would pay the money. At that time the Portugals and the Spaniards were held in respect for their rigid adherence to the code of honor which they had laid down for themselves.

The difficulty was to find a ship by which to send them, as the admiral was unwilling to go out of his course to land them. Hitherto the squadron had avoided all disaster, though not successful in making prizes. They were now in a part of the ocean where fearful hurricanes were at times to be expected, and in a latitude full of little-known islands and rocks; at the same time, they might hope to meet with numerous ships of the enemy.

Waymouth, as he thought on having to part with Donna Isabel so soon, became more and more downcast, though Edward and good Master Walker, the minister, and the other officers, did their utmost to keep up his spirits; some, like Raymond and Master Walker, by entering into his feelings; others, like Captain Wood, by bantering and quizzing.

"A sail! a sail!" was shouted from the masthead, whence a bright lookout was constantly kept. Chase was made—the stranger was overtaken. She proved to be a Portugal, a straggler from a large squadron supposed to be far ahead.

Not a moment was to be lost. Every article of value was taken from her except the fittings of her chief cabin, some guns for signals, and provisions sufficient to last her till she could reach the Malabar coast. The admiral then ordered the prisoners to be placed in her. Waymouth had the duty of conveying them.

Donna Isabel spoke but little, keeping her head muffled in her hood. The English lieutenant tried to talk, but never had he felt so tongue-tied. This was not surprising. He could say nothing definite about the future, and he had little to say about the past. He carefully helped her up the side, and placed her on a seat on the deck of the Tiger. Dom Joao was profuse in his expressions of gratitude for the treatment he and his daughter had received, and over and over again declared that it would afford him intense satisfaction to pay his ransom whenever demanded. Waymouth, like a true sailor, had hurried below to see what arrangements could be made for the comfort and convenience of Donna Isabel, and, having pointed out to the officers of the ship what was to be done, had returned on deck resolved to pour out all his feelings into her ear, when a gun from the admiral, repeated by the Lion, warned him that he must not delay another moment. All he could do was to bow low as he passed the lady and her father, utter a low farewell, and, leaping into his boat, pull back to the Lion as fast as his men could bend to their oars. The squadron instantly made all sail in chase of the enemy supposed to be ahead. For some time Waymouth had too much to do to look towards the ship on board which he had left the Portugal governor and his daughter, and when he did look she appeared but a speck on the horizon. He stood gazing, lost in a revery. He was aroused by a slap on the shoulder.

"Look ahead! that's the way we seamen set our faces," said a voice near him, "quoting your own words, coz. We have changed places, methinks."

Waymouth, looking round, saw Raymond and several other officers standing behind him. He heaved a sigh, and then joined in the laugh in which the rest were indulging. He had been too long at sea not to know the folly of growing angry under such circumstances. Besides, as he confessed to Raymond, he could not help feeling relieved at having no longer so important a charge. A brighter lookout than ever was kept on board the squadron, that they might not pass the enemy. Just before noon on the third day some strange sail were descried ahead. They increased in numbers: they were tall ships. There could be no doubt that they were those of the Portugal fleet they were in chase of, but far more numerous than they had been led to expect. Still undaunted, the brave admiral and his officers resolved to attack them. The Portugals saw the English approaching, and no longer, like caitiffs, flying before the foe, hauled their wind, and, forming a semicircle, prepared to receive them. In spite of the mighty superiority of the Portugals, the English sailed on in compact order, the men at their guns, their matches in their hands ready to open fire, every one in the fleet prepared for death or victory.

CHAPTER III.

The Portugal fleet, which the little English squadron was now rapidly approaching, looked formidable indeed, numbering as it did four times as many tall ships as the latter, but not a heart among the stout men who formed the crew of the Red Dragon, the Serpent, or the Lion, the Sunshine or Moonshine, quailed with the thoughts of combating against odds so great.

Good Master Walker, the minister of the Lion, went round among the crew as they stood at their quarters, reminding them that they were about to fight for their sovereign, their country, their honor, and their religion.

"And, dear lads," he added, "now is not the time to preach to you; but I have taught you all faithfully the truth, and would beseech all who have listened to remember and adhere by it."

The admiral had formed his line of battle, and, passing by each ship on his way to form the van, hailed through his speaking-trumpet, encouraging the crews to fight bravely for St. George and merry England, and promising them, if they gained the victory, the rich freights of all the ships they could capture. It was a bold feat of the gallant admiral thus to sail into the very midst of his foes, who he knew must surround him.

The Portugals were formed, as has been said, in a semicircle, with the concave side of their line turned toward the English, so that they might quickly overlap them — in a land fight an important point to gain, but at sea of slight advantage. The English were formed as a wedge; the Red Dragon led, the Serpent following, then came the two pinnaces, the Lion and Lion's Whelp bringing up the rear.

As the hostile fleets drew near, drums began to beat and trumpets to bray forth their discordant sounds, when, with a loud crashing roar, the artillery on both sides opened. The great guns sent forth their round shots, and the culverins, sakers, falconets, and murtherers their death-dealing showers of iron and lead, causing havoc and destruction wherever they fell. Ill pleased were the Portugals with this proceeding. Numbers were falling on board every ship. In vain they called on their saints to improve their aim and strengthen their powder — the shot seemed to have no effect on the heretical Englishmen — the saints paid them no attention. They had found a Tartar, and surrounded him, but were as disagreeably placed as if they had been dancing round an exploding magazine. Bravely plied the gallant English their guns. As long as any one of them had legs to stand on or arms to work with he refused to desert his quarters.

If one stopped for a moment from working his gun, it was to help a messmate bind a handkerchief round a wounded limb, or to tie one round his own leg or side. Officers and men vied with each other as to who should perform deeds most worthy of fame. The Portugals, on the contrary, though their trumpets brayed forth far louder than those of their foes, forgetful of their ancient renown, hastened below the instant they were wounded, however slight their hurts, crying out for the medico to come and help them; and some, when the English shots rattled on board, were seen to run away from their guns, even though unwounded. Still, numbers in so close a fight gave a great advantage to the Portugals.

The admiral's ship, the Red Dragon, especially was hard pressed, the enemy seeming resolved to destroy her first, hoping thus to gain an easy victory over the rest. But the brave Lancaster was not a man to be daunted. As fresh foes pressed around him he kept shouting to his crew —

"The more the merrier, lads! the more the merrier! We've pills enough on board to dose them all till they'll wish they'd come to some other doctor for their physic."

Captain Wood, too, was scarcely less hard pressed. He had sent the Lion's Whelp ahead to the support of the Sunshine and Moonshine, which seemed in danger of being altogether overwhelmed by the huge ships of the enemy which clustered around them, and thus the stout Lion had to encounter a whole host of foes by herself.

"Come one, come all!" shouted Captain Wood. "Brave lads, we are ready for them!"

"Ay, ay! one and all!" echoed Antony Waymouth. "Hurrah for merry England! Give it them, lads! A few more doses like that and they'll cry peccavi and strike their flags."

"Peccavimus you should have said," remarked Raymond, whom Waymouth was passing as he hurried from gun to gun to assure himself that all were being fought to the best advantage.

"Ay, marry, not one, but fifty, will sing that song to-day, coz," said Antony, laughing.

In truth, even in the heat of battle both officers and men indulged themselves in cutting jokes whenever an occasion occurred. Not, however, that the fight was any joking matter, for never in those seas had a more desperate one taken place. The brave men on board the Lion were falling thickly, some to rise no more, others to be carried below and placed in the hands of the surgeon, and to these Master Walker was rendering all the assistance in his power, and affording spiritual counsel and consolation at the same time. It was a dark, close place down in the depths of the ship, dimly lighted by two lanterns overhead, with a table in the centre and hammocks slung on either side, already occupied by wounded men. Others lay on the deck beneath, and one poor fellow was on the table, the surgeon and his assistants standing over him examining a dreadfully shattered limb. Master Walker was holding his hand and giving him some wine, of which, with vinegar and burnt feathers, the place was redolent, although they could not overcome that indescribable odor, dreadful and sickening, found wherever wounded men are collected together.

"It must be done, lad," said Master Walker kindly. "There's no help for it; the leg must come off to save thy life."

"What! lose my leg! never again to dance a hornpipe on Deerbrook Green among the lassies of our village? No more to come the double-shuffle and hear the merry clapping of the old people's hands? I'd as lief lose my life! But let the surgeon do his worst," murmured the lad, who was one of Waymouth's followers; "I'll bear it."

"Like a lion, I hope, lad," said the minister; "and pray to Heaven for strength — that's where you'll get the most."

"Seldom I've ever gone there for any thing," answered the lad with a sigh, and then, following the good minister, he endeavored to utter a prayer. It soon broke into groans, for the surgeons were operating on his limb, and these, in spite of his resolution, were succeeded by shrieks and cries, echoed by many of his poor shipmates who lay around him in the same sad plight. Not even the roar of the cannon overhead and the crashing of timbers, the shouts of the combatants and the rattle of the small arms, and the braying of the trumpets and other instruments, could altogether overpower those sad cries. Yet the sounds on deck grew louder and louder.

"There must be terrible work, I fear me, going on, Ap Reece," observed Master Walker to the Welsh surgeon, who had come round to feel the patient's wrist; "we've had no one brought down for the last five minutes."

The surgeon made no answer, but signed to the minister to pour some cordial down the young seaman's throat. "More — more! or he'll slip through our fingers," he whispered. The minister obeyed. The lad opened his eyes, and turning them towards him with an expression of gratitude, gasped out —

"Tell mother I've not forgotten fhe" —

A convulsive shudder passed over his frame, the blood started from beyond the tourniquet, and before the assistants could replace it the youth was a corpse.

"Peace be with him," said the minister solemnly, as the body was quickly removed to give place to another yet breathing victim of battle. Such is one of the many dark sides to the pictures of warfare. If this alone were to be seen, few would be eager for the combat.

"No more coming," once more observed the minister. "Either we must be hard pressed indeed, or have put the Portugals to flight."

"I fear me much the former," said Ap Reece. "I'd lief take a sword and go help our brave fellows. If the foe gain the day, they'll not leave one of us alive to tell the tale. What say you, Master Walker? will you come?"

"Nay, Ap Reece, abide where you are. Every man at his proper work — you tending the hurt, I speaking the truth to the salvation of their souls. Thus should we be found even were the end of the world approaching."

The high-spirited Welshman returned to his post, and though he had no more legs and arms to cut off, there was ample work for his skill. The dreadful uproar continued. It was evident that some of the enemy's ships had got alongside, and that the Lion's crew were engaged in repelling the Portugals who were attempting to board. Who was gaining the day it was impossible to say. It was a time truly of anxious suspense. Ap Reece could at length endure it no longer.

"If you go not on deck to learn how it fares with our men, Master Walker, I must go myself," he exclaimed; and, seeing that the minister did not move, he seized a sword which had been brought below by a wounded man, and sprang up the ladder. The chaplain looked hesitatingly in the same direction.

"No, no; my duty is with the suffering and dying, though I'd lief strike a blow as in days of yore for our reformed faith and merry England," said he to himself, and again turned to attend to a sorely wounded man by whose side he had been sitting.

Ap Reece soon gained the deck; he had been in many a fight, but never in a more desperate one. The Lion was closely surrounded by a forest of masts, with shattered spars, and burning sails, and severed ropes and blocks swinging to and fro, and splinters rattling from aloft, while round shots and bullets were flying thickly about, and from every side the loud clashing of steel showed that the combatants were striving hand to hand. The Portugals were attempting to board on every side of the Lion, but no sooner did they reach her deck than they were driven back with loss, and often followed on board their own ships. A new combatant had just come up on the Lion's quarter, and was pouring his crew on board. Waymouth caught sight of what was occurring, and with a handful of men sprang to repel the boarders. Hard pressed by the leader of the Portugals, he was well-nigh being driven back at the moment Ap Reece reached the deck. The surgeon saw at a glance where his services would be of most use, and shouting at the top of his voice a Welsh war-cry, he rushed to the lieutenant's assistance. Down before his sturdy blade went foe after foe till he reached Waymouth's side.

"A rescue! a rescue!" he shouted, and cleaving to the chin the head of one of the lieutenant's many assailants, the rest sprang hastily back, some into their own vessel, and some, missing their footing, overboard. "On, on!" shouted Waymouth. "On, on, and the enemy's ours!" cried Ap Reece; and following the retreating boarders they drove them across the deck of their ship, cutting down many, till the remainder cried out for quarter, when their flag was hauled down and the capture was complete.

"We have more prizes to make before the day is over, lads," cried Waymouth, and at that instant another large Portugal ship driving against the prize, he, with the brave Ap Reece and a number of followers, threw himself on her deck. So fierce was this onslaught that the enemy did not stand a moment, but tumbling below one over the other, or in their fright jumping overboard, or casting down their weapons, they allowed speedy possession to be taken of their ship. Waymouth and his companions then lashed the two prizes together, and not without difficulty regained the Lion, on the other side of which more of the enemy were congregated. Of one Captain Wood had taken possession. Waymouth and Ap Reece now sprang on board another about midships, when, dividing their forces, one swept forward and the other aft, driving their loudly vociferating foes before them till the Portugal's flag was hauled down.

"Hurrah! hurrah! my brave boys," shouted Waymouth. "Four prizes in the Lion's maw — the fattest in all the fleet, too, I have a notion — one more — yonder she comes. Strike fast, and strike home."

Thus shouting, he seized the helm of the prize, and steered her so as to fall foul of yet another big Portugal ship.

"Shall we once more tempt fortune?" cried Waymouth to the fighting surgeon. "What say you, Ap Reece? There must be ducats not a few aboard our tall friend here."

"But one answer to that question. On, on!" exclaimed the Welshman.

And no sooner did the sides of the two ships grind together than Waymouth lashed them by the shrouds, and then sprang on board the new-comer. She was full of men who showed every intention to defend her; but undaunted by numbers, the Englishmen threw themselves among them, with their sharp swords flashing rapidly, and soon hewed a lane for themselves from one side to the other. They had begun to cut a second when the Portugals, dreading the result, hauled down their own flag, and yielded. By this time such of the Portugal ships as were in a condition to escape were making the best of their way under all sail to the northward, leaving the rest in the hands of the English, who were in no condition to follow. The victors had indeed suffered severely, though it was some time before Waymouth, and those with him, could ascertain the true state of affairs. At length he brought his last-captured prize up to the Lion, where the rest were collected, and having secured his prisoners, and left a few men on board to watch them, he returned to his own ship. The Lion with her torn sails, shattered spars, and ropes hanging in disordered festoons, looked any thing but like a victor, yet she was in a better plight than her consorts. Far ahead lay the admiral with three of the enemy's ships he had captured, but his masts were tottering, and it was evident that he had suffered severely in the fight. The Serpent, though she had taken a couple of prizes, was even in a worse condition, while of the three smaller ships the poor little Moonshine had disappeared altogether, the Lion's Whelp lay a dismasted hulk on the waters, and the Sunshine appeared in a sinking condition. Three prizes, proofs of their prowess, lay near them, and it was to be hoped that some of the crew of the Moonshine had found safety on board them.

And now the surgeon, Ap Reece, his fiery blood beginning to cool, bethought him that he ought to go and look after his patients below, while Waymouth began to make inquiries as to who had been killed and who wounded among his shipmates. His grief was sincere when he heard of his young follower's death. He looked round, also, anxiously for Raymond. He was nowhere to be seen. Was he on board any of the prizes? No; such and such officers had charge of them. He sprang below. Master Walker could give him no tidings of his friend. He inquired eagerly of all the surviving officers. It was remembered that he had headed a party who had repulsed the boarders from a large Portugal ship, which had afterwards sheered off. Several men were missing who could not be accounted for, and it was supposed possible that he, with them, had gone on board the enemy, and that they had been carried off as prisoners. Waymouth hoped such might be the case, as it was the only chance of again seeing his friend, but, attached though he was to him, he had no time just then to mourn his loss.

Fearful had been the slaughter on board the Lion and the injuries she had received, while so many of her people had been taken off to man the prizes that not enough remained to repair the damages which she had received. The energies of every one on board unwounded were taxed to the utmost, nor could assistance be expected from the other ships, which had enough to do to look after their own prizes. The ships now closed up with each other, and the Lion was able to hail the admiral's ship.

"Sad news — sad news," was the answer. "Captain Lancaster was slain at the beginning of the fight, and though we have gained the victory we have bought it with the loss of half our men."

The loss on board the Serpent was also very great, though she had suffered less than the admiral's ship; but the Lion's Whelp and the Sunshine had lost, in proportion to their crews, as many men as the latter; while of the unfortunate Moonshine scarcely a third had escaped on board the prizes: all her wounded had gone down in her. The captain of the Serpent was also desperately wounded, and Captain Wood sent Waymouth on board to see him and receive his orders, as he was now chief in command. Waymouth, finding his way among the dying and wounded, reached the cockpit where Captain Nicholas Parker lay. He was groaning with anguish, which the surgeon, who stood by his side, was endeavoring to alleviate with a cordial. In vain. The groans continued, but grew fainter. The surgeon felt the captain's pulse. Waymouth stepped up.

"I have come to receive orders from the admiral, for such he now is, since Captain Lancaster has been killed," he said.

"Our brave captain will never give orders more," answered the surgeon with much feeling. "Your captain, Master Waymouth, will be admiral ere many minutes are over. We've gained victory at heavy cost."

Before Waymouth left the ship Captain Parker had breathed his last, and he pulled hastily back to announce the sad event to Captain Wood, who had now become commander-in-chief, but seemed but little elated with the circumstance. Master Walker was pacing the deck to recover from the effects of the close atmosphere he had endured below, and the harrowing scenes he had witnessed.

"This is what men call glory, and what young men sigh after and long to engage in," he observed, while Waymouth stood quiet for a few seconds discussing some food which had been brought to him, for he had no time to go below. "Look there; see what man's avarice and rage and folly have brought about in a few short hours."

He pointed with a melancholy glance at a number of slain arranged around the mainmast, and to several wounded who had been mercifully brought on deck to breathe a purer atmosphere than that to be found below; then to the Lion's shattered masts and bulwarks; and, lastly, moving his hand round to their almost dismasted, and yet more shattered, consorts and prizes, from one of which, taken by the Serpent, at that instant flames were seen to burst forth. The Lion had but one boat which could float, and into her an officer and crew jumped and pulled away to the assistance of the burning vessel, the men being urged to speed, not impossibly, in the hope of obtaining some of the plunder on board.

The Serpent had sent off two of her boats, and the Red Dragon another, but the Portugals either would not go to the assistance of their countrymen or their boats were knocked to pieces, or the officers in charge of the prizes would not let them go, for no assistance was sent, though several were near the burning vessel. The boats pulled rapidly through the water; and good cause they had so to do, for the flames rose higher and higher, bursting out from all the ports from stem to stern till there appeared not a spot on which a human being could stand unscorched by the fire. Busily as all on board the Lion were employed, they stopped to gaze on the scene. Even amid the flames they could see the unhappy men rushing here and there, seeking in vain for safety: some were casting themselves into the sea; others, unable probably to swim, waited anxiously for the boats. In vain! in vain! Ere the boats reached them the burning masts and spars rose gradually up from the hull — up, up, they shot into the air; the deck followed, the flames increasing with tenfold fury, a loud report announcing that the magazine had exploded, and that the rich argosy, with all still living on board, had been hurried to destruction. Those in the boats pulled back, endeavoring to avoid the burning fragments of spars and wreck which came hissing in a thick shower around them. Then recollecting that some might yet be floating near where the wreck had been, like true British tars they again dashed on, in the hope of rescuing them. So rapidly had the catastrophe occurred after the first outbreak of the fire, that Waymouth had not moved from the minister's side.

"There, there!" continued the latter, "surely such work as that is the invention of Satan — that roaring lion who is ever going about seeking whom he may devour. What mad folly in men thus to yield to him, and to destroy each other at his will and beck!"

"What you say, Master Walker, may be true —

all very true; but we are in for it, and must carry through our enterprise, or perish," exclaimed Waymouth, with rather more impatience than he was wont to address the minister. "We have taken prizes enough to make every man of us wealthy for the rest of our lives; but our loss of brave fellows has been heavy, I grant you, and I'd give up every ducat that falls to my share for the sake of knowing what has become of Edward Raymond, and all the gold I may ever possess to get him back safe aboard here."

"He was a worthy gentleman, and I pray that he may still be reckoned among the living," said the chaplain, and he was about to commence an exhortation to his young friend when Waymouth was called away to attend to one of the numberless duties which, in consequence of the loss of many of his messmates, now fell to his lot.

As soon as shot-holes had been plugged, the wounded masts and spars strengthened, the shrouds set up, and damaged rigging repaired, an examination of the prizes commenced. The wealth they contained surpassed even the expectation of the adventurers. Besides gold and silver in bars, there were cases of diamonds and pearls and other precious stones, and casks and cases of rich spices, and strange and rich silks, and a variety of other articles from India. In truth, there appeared to be more than enough to enrich even the commonest seaman of the squadron, although by far the largest share would go to the officers.

Fortunately, the weather remained calm, or more of the ships would have gone to the bottom. Every one exerted himself to the utmost, and good reason he had so to do, for a storm might arise, or the enemy return with greater force, and all the treasure gained by so much toil and bloodshed might be lost.

Before the day was over, the signal was made from the Serpent that Captain Parker had ceased to breathe. Captain Wood therefore assumed the chief command, and ordered the Red Dragon to come near that he might go on board her, leaving Waymouth in command of the Lion.

A consultation of all the chief officers was now held, and it was determined to abandon and destroy the Sunshine and Lion's Whelp, to shift their crews on board the two largest and least injured of the Portugal ships, to select a third on board which to put all the prisoners, and to burn the remainder. The plan was at once put into execution, and the wealth of all her prizes was carried on board the Lion. Not, however, till two days had passed were the prizes sufficiently gutted of their stores and provisions to be abandoned. A short time before nightfall they were set on fire; and it was a sad though a fine sight to see eight tall ships burning away together. Master Walker again had reason to shake his head.

"Another example of man's folly," he exclaimed. "See yon beautiful fabrics, on which so much thought, time, and labor was expended, being destroyed in a few short minutes!"

"But you would not have us tow the useless hulls round the world, Master Walker, would you?" asked Waymouth, with some little hastiness not to be wondered at."

"No, Captain Waymouth, but I would that the hulls were not useless, and still freighted with honest merchandise, that we and the Portugals were at peace, as Christian men should be, and each pursuing our own course as gentlemen adventurers for our own profit and advantage and that of our respective countries. When I joined the expedition I understood such was to be the case. We were to be armed to resist attack, as is lawful — not to attack others, which is wrong. But all these doings of blood and destruction have opened my eyes, and made me wish that I had remained quiet at home, even though my stipend was small and precarious. I love you right well, as you of a surety do know, Captain Waymouth, and I tell you that no good can come of these doings.

"I see not the strength of your reasoning, Master Walker," said Waymouth. "We all know when we left Old England that we were embarking in an adventure in which we should meet with hard blows as well as rich prizes. We are in no wise worse than Drake, and see what honors have been heaped on him."

"I say nothing against the powers that be; and

her gracious majesty may have had her reasons for honoring Sir Francis; but there are persons who consider his expedition round the world as worthy only of a sea-rover of old or of a downright pirate," observed the minister.

"Let be, let be, Master Walker," exclaimed Waymouth petulantly; "I can brook more from you than from any man alive, but I have heard enough."

The minister was too wise to proceed, but he shook his head mournfully.

The prisoners were now all collected on board one ship. Among the wild spirits found among the English crews some were not wanting who suggested that they should be sent adrift without compass, guns, or provisions; some even hinted that to bore holes in the ship's bottom would be the surest way of disposing of them; others considered that it would be wise to keep them as prisoners, and to insure their keeping with the fleet they should only be furnished day by day with the necessary provisions, and that two ships should be appointed especially to watch them. More generous counsels, however, prevailed.

"No, no, by my halidom!" exclaimed Captain Wood; "Portugals though they are, they have fought bravely, and like honest gentlemen shall be treated. We'll give them arms to defend their lives, and provisions to fill their insides, and a compass to find their way to some one of their own ports or factories on the coast of the Indies, and all we'll demand of them is that if they find any Englishmen in the same plight as they are themselves that they treat them in the same way as they are treated by us."

Waymouth warmly seconded the admiral's proposal; so did several of the superior officers, though others grumbled at letting the prisoners off without a ransom, or trusting to their honor to return the favor they were to receive.

Away sailed the Portugal ship with all the prisoners on board; not, however, without Waymouth having extracted a promise from all the officers to make inquiries for his friend Raymond, and to let him know, if alive, where he was to be found. Waymouth hoped that among them some at least would do their utmost to redeem their promise.

Once more the English fleet was sailing proudly over the seas, but sadly diminished in the number of their men. The wealth collected seemed prodigious in the eyes of the crews, and little short of that obtained by Drake of the Spaniards. Still their success only made them greedy for more, and the seamen especially expressed their aversion to the trading part of the enterprise, and loudly proclaimed their desire to cruise against any enemy to be found—Dutch, if Portugals could not be found, or Spaniards if they could be fallen in with. Waymouth, especially, found that he had a very mutinously inclined crew to deal with. Who was the chief instigator he determined to discover, in the hope that by punishing him he might bring the rest under better discipline.

The officer next in command to him was Miles Carlingford, an honest, straight-forward seaman, on whom he knew that he could depend as well as he could on Master Walker and the surgeon Ap Reece as to faithfulness; but Master Walker was a non-combatant, and would be averse to any stringent measures; and Ap Reece, from his hot-headed impetuosity, would be likely to betray any counsel with which he was intrusted.

Captain Wood had brought two cabin-boys with him — or, as they would now be called, midshipmen — and these he had left under Waymouth's especial care. Poor fellows! early indeed were they to be initiated into the stern realities of life. It would have been difficult to find a stronger contrast than between the two lads, and yet they were great friends. The eldest, Alfred Stanhope, was of high birth, of which he was fully conscious. He was refined in appearance and manners, and was light-hearted and gay in the extreme. He was never out of spirits or out of humor, and was utterly indifferent to danger. His talents, however, were not great, and the knowledge he did possess was very superficial. His father was a spendthrift and a ruined man, and had allowed him to come to sea in the hope of his being provided for in one way or another.

His companion, Oliver Marston, was the son of a

stout English yeoman to whom Captain Wood's family was under some obligations, and, as a way of repaying him, he had offered to take Oliver, one of ten sons, on an adventure through which he would be certain to secure his fortune. The lad, though he had never seen a ship except worked on tapestry, had no objection to go to sea. He was a short, stout, strongly-built little fellow, able to hold his own with all competitors. While poor Alfred Stanhope had been nurtured in the lap of luxury, Oliver had been brought up in the roughest style, and was therefore much better able than his companion to buffet with the storms of life they were doomed to encounter. He had much more sense and shrewdness in his round little head than might have been supposed, while all about him was sterling stuff of the toughest nature, except his heart, in one respect, and that was as soft and gentle as that of a true sailor is said to be. Oliver was a favorite with Waymouth, who, though he did not spoil him, encouraged him to speak more openly to him than he allowed any one else to do except Master Walker.

It was night. Waymouth was seated in his cabin. A lamp hung from the beam above, the light of which fell on a chart he was anxiously scanning. Unwonted cares oppressed even his buoyant spirit. His ship had suffered much; he had a large amount of wealth on board; his crew was much weakened, some were disaffected, and he was about to enter

seas difficult of navigation, and where typhoons might be expected. He mourned, too, his friend Raymond's loss, though he did not believe that he was dead, but that he had been carried off a prisoner by the enemy. Still, how could he hear of him, and how rescue him if he was a prisoner? He fell into a revery. He was aroused by the sentry at the announcement that an officer wished to see him.

"Let him come," was the answer; and Oliver Marston stood before him.

"What now, Oliver?" asked the captain.

"You know, Captain Waymouth, that I am not a tale-bearer; but I've just heard some matters which I bethought me I ought to convey to you without delay," answered Marston. "There's mutiny in the ship, sir, or what may come to worse."

"Ah! how come you to know that, boy?" asked the captain anxiously, for the announcement somewhat confirmed his own suspicions.

The youngster answered promptly — "It is my first watch, sir, and as I had no fancy for turning in for a short time, I lay down for a snooze on a chest outside the boatswain's cabin. I was afraid of oversleeping myself, so quickly awoke, and was about to jump up, when I heard voices near me. The words were spoken in an undertone, as if the speakers desired not to be overheard. Who the speakers were, I am not certain; they talked of the wealth that was on board, and how you and the other captains would get the lion's share, but that if they acted with spirit and stuck together they might have the whole of it."

"And you heard the whole of this, and were not dreaming, boy?"

"Every word, sir, and I was wide awake," answered Oliver.

"You have done well to come to me at once," said the captain. "Speak to no one of what you have heard, and appear even to your messmates as if all were going on right. To-morrow morning I will communicate with the admiral, and we will soon have these would-be mutineers in limbo. Have you no idea who were the speakers?"

"I like not, sir, to bring an accusation against any man without perfect certainty, but to the best of my belief there were Peter Hagger, the boatswain, and John Moss, his mate, among the chief speakers," answered Oliver. "As to the rest I might be mistaken, but I think not of those two. I recognized also Dick Soper's voice, and he is not likely to be left out if such work is proposed."

"He'll swing ere long at the yard-arm, an' I mistake not; but enough now, lad," said the captain. "Keep counsel and your eyes about you, and we'll defeat the rebels. They'll attempt nothing while we are with the admiral; they know him, and I thought they knew me too. Who has the first watch?"

"Mr. Carlingford, sir," said Marston.

"Tell him to keep close up with the admiral, as I want to speak him at dawn," said Waymouth; "and call me should the weather give signs of change. You have acted most commendably."

The lad took his leave well pleased with the praise bestowed on him by his captain, and very indifferent to the danger to which he as well as all the officers on board were exposed.

The young captain sat for some time meditating on the matter. He could not tell how many of the crew might be engaged in the plot, and on what support the conspirators depended. He might discover who were the ringleaders, but find that the greater part of the crew sided with them. Caution, courage, and decision would be required—he trusted he should not be wanting in either of the three. The last few days had been a time of unusual exertion and care. He required rest to restore his well-nigh exhausted energies. Examining his firearms with more care than usual, and placing his sword by his side ready for instant use, though he firmly believed that no attempt would be made by the mutineers, he threw himself on his bed. He had resolved to take the Lion next morning under the guns of the Red Dragon, and having informed Captain Wood of what he knew, call out the three men whose voices young Marston recognized, and send them on board the flagship for punishment. He soon, however, forgot his anxieties in a sound sleep.

He was awoke by the voice of Oliver Marston loudly calling him.

"What is it?" he asked, starting up with his sword grasped in his hand.

CHAPTER IV.

"What is it?" exclaimed the young captain of the Lion, as he sprang from his bed, on which he had thrown himself without undressing. He did not require the cabin-boy's answer, for by the way the ship was heeling over he knew that it was blowing a heavy gale. "I bade you call me the instant there were signs of a change of weather," he observed as he hurried towards the cabin-door to gain the deck.

"The ship but this instant was struck by a squall, sir, and we are shortening sail as fast as we can," said Marston, though the captain did not stay to hear his last words.

The deck of the Lion appeared, as the captain reached it, to be a scene of the greatest confusion. Showers of spray, torn up from the ocean by the sudden squall, were thrown over her in dense masses. The wind howled and whistled through the rigging, the sales were flapping loudly in the gale — some torn from their bolt-ropes, others with the sheets let go, which were lashing and slashing wildly and twisting into a thousand knots. Huge blocks, too, were swinging to and fro, threatening the seamen with destruction, while some of the spars wounded in the action now gave way, and their fragments came thundering down on deck, sweeping all before them. The sea roared, the thunder in crashing peals rattled along the sky, and the forked lightning ran hissing in vivid flashes from out of the dark clouds along the foaming waves, and played round the ship. The officers were shouting to the men — many, with axes and knives in their hands, rushing here and there at the risk of their lives to cut clear the blocks and the wreck of the spars, without which it was scarcely possible to go aloft to furl the remaining sails.

Waymouth at once saw that the only safe course to pursue was to put the ship before the wind. As he issued the required orders he looked out for the admiral's ship, but the signal lanterns at her stern were nowhere to be seen. Mr. Carlingford asserted that they were close to them when the squall struck the ship; so did Stanhope, who did the duty of a signal midshipman. The captain could only hope, therefore, that the admiral had at once bore up when the hurricane struck his ship. Two lights were still visible in the direction the other ships were supposed to be, but at some distance, and the Lion was apparently fast leaving them. Her crew had indeed enough to do to attend to themselves — their own safety demanded all their energies. Waymouth's firm, commanding voice soon called order out of chaos. The ship answered her helm, and, getting before the wind once more, rose on an even keel, and flew rushing on through the darkness. Sail after sail was taken in — the loftier masts and spars had been carried away by the wind, and were mostly cut clear of the ship. The foretopmast had escaped being hit in the action, and had stood. The hurricane was increasing in power, rolling up the ocean into huge seas; higher and higher they grew, their crests curling masses of foam, following eagerly astern as wild beasts in pursuit of their flying prey. Often, while the forked lightning played round the ship, had the captain gazed anxiously at the foretopmast to ascertain how it stood the increasing pressure deprived of its usual support. He scarcely hoped to save it. The hurricane gave no signs of abating; on the contrary, it was increasing in strength.

"It must be done!" he exclaimed, seizing a sharp axe; "better choose our time than let it fall when we are unprepared. Volunteers to cut away the foretopmast!"

"I'll go," cried Miles Carlingford, and his words were echoed by several others.

"No, Carlingford; you stay to take care of the ship. I can let no man lead but myself in a task of such peril."

Marston and Stanhope both volunteered, but the captain ordered them to remain with the lieutenant.

Followed by a daring crew, Waymouth sprang aloft, each man armed with axe or knife. Some remained on deck to cut the ropes which led down there. All had their tasks assigned them. The least important ropes and stays were first severed.

"Remember, lads, wait till I give the word, and then cut with a will," cried the captain. As he stood on the top his axe was lifted in the air. "Cut!" he shouted, as, gleaming in the lightning, it descended with a force which half severed through the spar. Over it fell with a crash into the sea, and, free from all ropes, floated clear of the ship. The crew uttered a hearty cheer as the captain descended on deck after the performance of this gallant and skilful act without the loss of a man. None cheered more loudly than the boatswain and his two mates.

The ship drove on before the hurricane, but, relieved of so much top hamper, she labored far less than she had been doing. The storm had not abated its fury; the mad waves followed fiercely after the ship, and leaped up, foam-covered, on either side, threatening to fall down on her decks and sweep everybody from off them, or to send the stout bark herself to the bottom. The thunder roared loudly as at first, the lightning flashed vividly as ever, and ran its zigzag course crackling and hissing through the air, and along the summits of the waves, and round the storm-driven ship, now seeming to dart along her spars, and then to light with a lambent flame the summit of her masts.

The crew were collected on deck ready for any work required of them, sheltering themselves as best they could under the bulwarks for fear of being washed away. Waymouth stood with his first lieutenant on the aftercastle away from the crew. He told him of the conspiracy of which he had gained information.

"What think you, Carlingford?" he added. "Shall we seize the villains now, tax them with their intended crime, and call on all who are for discipline and order to rally round us; or let them go on plotting till they find a fit occasion to put their plots into execution? It were a bold stroke at such a moment, and would be sure of success."

"No one would be found willing to differ from you now," answered the lieutenant; "I doubt, therefore, that you would ascertain who are the conspirators, and it would only give them a certain vantage-ground by showing them that you doubt their honesty."

Waymouth yielded to this advice, and allowed the opportunity of seizing the supposed mutineers to pass. He had no fear that they would make any attempt to gain possession of the ship while the gale might last. In spite of the danger in which his own ship was placed, he turned his thoughts more than once to the rest of the squadron. What had become of them? Were they still afloat, driven here and there before the hurricane, or had they all met the fate from which the Lion herself had so narrowly escaped, and foundered? He could not help dreading that the latter might have been the case.

Hour after hour passed by, and the wind blew fiercely as at the commencement of the storm. No fire could be lighted. Scarcely any one had even tasted food, and the fierce spirits who had been before inclined to mutiny must have been considerably tamed by the buffeting and fasting they had been compelled to undergo.

"I've heard say that it's an ill wind that blows no one good," observed Carlingford to his captain. "I doubt if the knaves who so notably were proposing to take possession of the ship will be inclined to make the attempt for some time to come."

"We will keep an eye on them, at all events," said Waymouth. "In the present battered condition of our good ship, they will be too wise to wish to run away with her, or all the labor of putting her to rights would fall on their hands. Ah, no, the rogues! they will let us first do the work for them, and then cut our throats. I have met before with villains such as these, and know how to tackle them."

Although occasionally brave villains are found, as a rule ill-doers are cowards; and the would-be mutineers on board the Lion were no exception to the rule. The captain and his lieutenant noted those who on that awful night showed most fear, and they proved to be the very men Marston had mentioned. Even the boatswain, who was generally a bold fellow, evidently shrank from the performance of any duty of especial danger, and while the captain went aloft to cut away the topmast was not one of those who had volunteered to accompany him, though under ordinary circumstances it would have been his duty to perform the work.

Morning broke at length upon the wide waste of foam-covered heaving waters, but in vain did the anxious officers of the Lion look around for any of her consorts. She herself was laboring heavily. The well was sounded. There were three feet of water in the hold; that was much in a ship of the Lion's build. There must be a leak. The pumps were manned; all hands must work spell and spell. Even then scarcely could the leak be kept under. Those men who had shown the greatest courage during the night labored the hardest now; the conspirators worked with an air of desperation.

When the water still gained on them, "Let's to the spirit-room, and die jovial," cried one.

"Ay, ay, to the spirit-room; a last glass before we quit the world," was echoed by several.

Deserting their stations, they rushed tumultuously to the hold. They found three soldiers stationed there, with their muskets ready to fire. Strange that the very men who were about to stupefy themselves with liquor, and so to go out of the world, were afraid of dying by the hands of their countrymen! Growling like cowed mastiffs they shrank back, some returning to the deck, and others turning into their hammocks, where they intended to remain while the ship sank.

But a few only behaved thus. The greater number, as true British seamen always have done, remained at their posts to face the danger. Their perseverance was rewarded. About noon the gale began to abate, the sea to decrease. As the ship labored less there was a hope that the leaks might be got under, and the carpenters, after sounding, reported that there was not more than the usual quantity of water in the well. The news was received with loud cheers by the crew, but they soon found that continued exertion would be necessary to keep the ship afloat. The skulkers were accordingly routed out of their berths, and compelled to take their turn at the pumps.

Waymouth well knew that idleness is the mother of many a crime, and he determined that his crew should have no such excuse. As soon as the sea became calm, there was ample work to employ all hands in repairing the damages the ship had received in the battle and the storm.

"Any day we may meet an enemy, and the ship must be in a state to fight him, lads," the captain was continually remarking, especially when he saw the men slacken at their work. A course had been shaped for the Island of Java, where in the Harbor of Bantam he still entertained hopes of falling in with the rest of the squadron.

Day after day the Lion continued her voyage without further adventure, and every day saw some advance made in restoring her to her former condition, so that, had she encountered a Portugal ship, she would have been as ready as ever for the fight.

In appearance, however, she still wore a very battered and forlorn state. Such was the guise in which she at length entered the harbor of Bantam, making the best show that was possible, with banners and streamers flying, and drums and fifes, and other music, playing. Very different, however, was the figure they made from what they had expected, and what it would have been, had the whole English squadron sailed in at the same time. Very different also was the reception they received from the King of Bantam, in those days a powerful sovereign with a magnificent court of nobles dressed in rich robes. Perceiving the coldness of their reception, Waymouth, habiting himself in his most imposing attire, and taking a number of followers, attired in all the bravery they could command, went on shore, and, on obtaining admission to the palace, informed his majesty that his ship was only the first of a large fleet which had just obtained a glorious victory over the Portugals, and that he hoped they would soon enter the harbor and spend a large portion of their wealth among him and his people. When this fact became clear to the royal mind, the king's conduct underwent a considerable alteration, and he seemed now only anxious to ascertain how he could best please his guests. There was no lack of entertainments of all sorts — fights of wild animals, shows, and dances. These served to amuse the men, and to prevent them from thinking of the future. But Waymouth and his chief officers could not get rid of their anxiety for their companions. They still, however, lived on in hopes. In the mean time, the captain's chief uneasiness arose from the conduct of the boatswain, who was clearly endeavoring to ingratiate himself with the crew by overlooking their faults and shielding them from punishment. The consequence was that the discipline of the ship, spite of all the captain and superior officers could do to prevent it, became worse than it had ever been before. Miles Carlingford advised Waymouth to have Hagger and his supposed associates seized, and run up to the yard-arm, or shot; but there were many reasons against this summary proceeding. They were in the port of a treacherous people, who would very likely take advantage of any dissensions among themselves, and it was impossible to say how many of the crew might join Hagger.

"We must either wait the arrival of the rest of the fleet or seize the fellow in blue water, with no one to interfere with us," answered Waymouth.

However, day after day passed by, and week after week, and the fleet did not appear. It became at last too probable that they had all foundered. Still it was possible that they might have put into some other port to refit, and might arrive at the rendezvous after all.

The time passed pleasantly enough on shore, as great respect was shown to the strangers by the king and chiefs. The English, in return, tried to make themselves popular with all classes, and traded successfully with them, taking care not to allow them to know the amount of wealth they had on board. Hope grew meantime fainter and fainter, and it struck Waymouth that the behavior of the natives towards them had of late changed for the worse. Among the merchants with whom he had dealings was one who appeared to be especially honest, and more disposed to be friendly than any of his countrymen. One day he made his appearance on board, saying that he had come to trade, and he began in the usual way, but while so engaged he contrived with a peculiar gesture to give a paper to Waymouth, on which was drawn a ship under full sail. Above the ship was a hand, showing the very gesture the merchant had just made. Waymouth could scarcely fail to understand the hieroglyphic. That the merchant wished the Lion to sail away there could be no doubt. The expression of the man's countenance convinced him that he was friendly and in earnest. Some danger threatened. Perhaps the king had got information of the wealth contained in the ship, and intended to seize her. Whatever enemies they might have on shore, there was one who could not be kept out of the ship. The unhealthy season was approaching. Fever made its appearance on board; several were struck down with it; one after the other died; the surgeon declared that the only way of saving the lives of all on board was to put forthwith to sea.

Once more the Lion was ploughing the waters of the deep. "A sail! a sail!" was the cry. A vessel was seen making for the harbor of Bantam. She might be one of the long-missing squadron. Sail was made in chase. As the Lion approached, the stranger showed the Portugal flag. Hurrah! another prize was to be made. The thought put every one in high spirits. Even the sick came up from their beds to have a look at the enemy. The object of the Portugal was to enter the harbor of Bantam before the Lion, under the belief that he would there find protection. On sprang the king of beasts. It soon became obvious, unless there was a change of wind, that the prey would have little chance of escape. The officers and crew of the Lion eagerly watched the Portugal ship, speculating on the value of her cargo, and whether she was likely to offer resistance. Such an idea was generally treated with scorn. What was the surprise, therefore, of all on board to see the chase suddenly haul up her courses and heave her maintopsail aback to await the coming of her pursuer!

"Can it be that any on board are treacherous, and wish thus to gain our favor?" said Waymouth.

"More likely that they are cowards all, and think

discretion the best part of valor," observed Carlingford; "we shall soon learn, though."

"Ay, that shall we," answered Waymouth. "But, see, what flags are those? They look not as if the Portugal was in a humble mood."

As he was speaking, several flags were hoisted to the mastheads of the stranger, conspicuous among all being that of Portugal flying above the flag of England. The sight caused a general shout of indignation among the English crew, and doubled their desire to get alongside the foe. As they got still nearer, the Portugal once more let fall his sails and stood boldly towards them, letting fly a shot in defiance.

"Now this is what does the heart good," exclaimed Waymouth in high glee. "Yonder is a brave fellow and a worthy foe. I had ten times rather meet such a one than the coward who runs away and then yields when he is caught without striking a blow. We shall take yonder gentleman — of that there is no doubt; and it will be a satisfaction to treat him as a brave man should be treated — with honor and distinction."

"I would that we could avoid fighting," said Master Walker. "Here are we both from Europe — two ships, the remnant, probably, of the proud fleets which left our native shores — and we must needs set to work to knock each other to pieces. What, prithee, is to be gained by it?"

"Honor, good Master Walker! honor, which we

gentlemen of the sword sigh for and live for, not to speak of the golden doubloons and other articles of value with which these Portugals think fit to freight their ships," answered Waymouth with a laugh which showed the cool if not light spirit with which he could enter into the deadly fight.

Nearer and nearer drew the two ships. The Portugal was the first to fire, and all his guns were aimed high, as if he was anxious to cripple his opponent. The reason was obvious. His decks were crowded with men, and he hoped by running on board the English ship to take her easily with his overwhelming numbers. Waymouth saw that his proper plan was to give the Portugals a wide berth and keep firing away till he had thinned those numbers, at the same time that it was very much against his usual system and inclination, as it was against that of his followers.

Now the guns of the Lion began to play vigorously, some of them being, according to the captain's orders, fired high, and others low. Although now and then her spars and ropes were hit, she was inflicting equal injury on the rigging of her opponent, while such of her guns as were trained low were making fearful havoc among the people on the deck of the Portugal. She, in return, was employing every manœuvre to close with the Lion, till it appeared as if the English were actually afraid of her.

"This must not last longer," exclaimed Waymouth. "British steel has seldom failed, however great the odds. We'll give the Portugals their way."

The remark was received with a loud shout by his men, on which he ordered the Lion to be steered to close with her antagonist. The two ships met with a crash; and before the Portugals, who had been mustering on purpose, could reach the side of the Lion, her gallant crew, led by Waymouth, had boarded the enemy. And now, in truth, was shown what English steel could do; and well as many of the Portugals fought, the decks were soon cleared of all but a gallant few, who, surrounding the Portugal captain, stood at bay. That Portugal captain was a young man of a noble bearing; though wounded, he seemed resolved to resist to the last.

"Yield thee — yield thee, brave senhor!" cried Waymouth. "Life and liberty shall be yours. I would fain not kill thee."

"To you, brave Captain Waymouth, I will yield me, if you will order your men to refrain from striking," was the answer. "Truly, they strike so hard and fast, that otherwise not one of my comrades will remain alive."

"You are a brave gentleman. It shall be as you desire. We have met before, I suspect," shouted the English captain, ordering his men to let drop the points of their weapons.

The deck, so lately the scene of a fierce conflict,

was in an instant quiet, though the planks, slippery with gore, and the human forms strewed thickly from one end to the other, showed the desperate nature of the drama which had there been enacted. The Portugal captain delivered his sword to Waymouth, who courteously returned it, recognizing him as the bravest of those captains who had been captured in the great battle fought by the whole fleet — Don Antonio de Mello by name. The prize was richly freighted, and as the Lion would require some repairs after the battle, it was resolved to carry her back to Bantam.

The return of the English so soon with a captured enemy raised them very much in the estimation of the people of Bantam, and proportionately lowered the Portugals. The repairs of both ships were soon completed, and the more valuable part of the cargo of the prize transferred to the Lion. Waymouth's generous feelings prompted him to restore the captured ship to Don Antonio, taking his word that neither he nor his officers or men would again serve against the English. He made the proposal, however, first to his own officers, who all, with the exception of Peter Hagger, readily agreed to forego their share of the prize that the prisoners might have an opportunity of returning to their own country. The boatswain, on the contrary, vowed, that, as they had won the booty by hard fighting, they would keep it, and that he and many other good men that he knew of would not give up a nail of what was their own.

"Well said, Master Hagger; let me know who are these good men of whom you speak, and your share and theirs of what is restored to the Portugals shall be calculated and given to you," said Captain Waymouth, looking sternly at the boatswain. "I wish to deprive no man of what he considers his own; but it strikes me that when a fair estimate is made of the real value of your share it will not be worth disputing about."

Notwithstanding these remarks of the captain, Hagger insisted on having his share, but he was only able to send in the names of rather more than a dozen men who agreed with him. The supercargo, or accountant, of the Lion, was therefore summoned, and directed to make out an estimate of the value of the shares in question.

"Now deduct therefrom," said Waymouth, "wages of officers and crew of the Portugal to conduct her home; risk of capture or loss; increased risk of loss or capture of the Lion in consequence of her being short-handed."

"In that case, sir, the balance is against Master Hagger and the rest," remarked the accountant.

"I thought as much," observed Waymouth, laughing.

The boatswain's anger and disappointment were very great when he found how the tables had been turned, and that, instead of gaining any thing, he had merely shown who were the men among the crew plotting with him.

The Portugals' satisfaction was very great when they found that they were not to be detained at Bantam, where, from the unhealthiness of the climate during the hot months, they could expect only to find graves. Don Antonio warmly expressed his gratitude.

"I had some information, noble captain, which I purposed giving before parting, at all events, but which I have now a double gratification in affording," he said, addressing Waymouth. "During that dreadful fight, when your fleet destroyed so many of ours, some few Englishmen were carried off prisoners by those which escaped. Among them was an officer who belonged to the Lion. I saw him but once, and his name I did not hear, though I doubt not that he is the friend whose fate you so much desired to learn. He is now a prisoner in the Castle of San Pedro, to the south of Goa. I had resolved to take the earliest opportunity of sending you this information according to my promise, little supposing that I should be able to deliver it under, to me, such unfortunate circumstances."

This news raised Waymouth's spirits higher than they had been for some time. It made him feel almost sure that Raymond had survived the battle, because, as all the other officers of the Lion had been accounted for, it could be only him of whom Don Antonio spoke. On hearing this, it at once flashed across Waymouth's thoughts that he had done unwisely in giving the prisoners their liberty with so few conditions.

"I ought to have bargained that any English who might be in the hands of their countrymen should promptly be liberated without ransom; but yet — no; I have done a liberal deed, and I will not regret it. If these Portugals have any feeling of honor, they will let my friend go free when I demand him."

From a subsequent conversation with Don Antonio, Waymouth was compelled to abandon the last expressed hope. It appeared that the governor of the castle of San Pedro was a certain Don Lobo, who was noted for his ferocity and avarice, so that he was well called Lobo, which means in the Portugal tongue a wolf.

Don Antonio stated that he was never known to do a noble or generous act, and that he was not likely to deliver up his prisoner unless a heavy ransom was paid, and that so bitter was his animosity against the English that it was possible he would not even set him at liberty.

"Then the Lion shall force the wolf to succumb," exclaimed Waymouth. "I will not ask you, Don Antonio, to fight against your countrymen, but I must beg you to give me such information as may assist me in liberating my friend, and I must then exact a promise from you that you will not return to San Pedro, or by any means allow notice of our approach to be carried there."

Don Antonio, without hesitation, gave the promise required, the more readily, perhaps, that the Lion would have the start of him for some days, and, being short of provisions and water, he could not attempt to make so long a passage as that from Bantam to Goa without being amply supplied with both. Yet further to prevent the chance of Don Lobo being informed of the approach of the Lion, Waymouth afterwards extracted an additional promise from Don Antonio that he would not attempt to sail for a week after her.

"Ned, dear coz, we shall once more shake hands, and drink a bowl together to the health of thy lady love," he exclaimed, apostrophizing his friend while walking his quarter-deck, as the Lion, under all sail, clove her way towards the west through the limpid ocean.

CHAPTER V.

Our chronicle takes us back to the time when the fight between the English and Portugal fleets was raging most furiously, and when, to an inexperienced eye like that of Edward Raymond, on finding his ship surrounded, it might naturally have appeared that victory was siding with his foes rather than with his own party. He believed, however, that by a desperate effort the day might be retrieved, and he gallantly resolved on his part to make the effort, trusting that others would be doing the like at the same moment. Just then he caught sight of Waymouth repelling the boarders from one of the Portugal ships, and so calling on all the men near to follow, he led them on to the deck of another of the enemy's ships which had at that moment run alongside. So fierce was his attack, that the foe gave way, and before many minutes were over he found himself master of the ship; but in the mean time she had broken clear of the Lion, and was drifting down on another Portugal ship coming freshly into the fight. The two were soon locked together, and while he with his handful of followers was endeavoring to defend his prize at one end of the ship, a party of Portugals rushed on board at the other. In vain he fought with the greatest heroism. Most of his followers were cut down. Pressed on all sides, he had not a prospect of success. Another Portugal ship came up. His prize, so gallantly taken, was already recaptured. Unable to parry a stroke made at him, he was severely wounded, and dropping the point of his sword, he yielded himself a prisoner to the reiterated demands of a Portugal captain who had headed the chief body of his assailants. The three Portugal ships had, however, fallen within the fire of the Red Dragon and the Serpent, whose shot crashing on board made them glad to set all the sail they could spread and draw off. As Edward stood on the deck and saw the shattered condition of the English ships, he could scarcely believe that the enemy were really drawing off; but when he afterwards saw some of the Portugals actually sinking, and others with their masts gone, he could not refrain from uttering a cheer, faint though it was, at the thought that his countrymen had gained the hard-fought victory. In this he was joined by the few survivors of his brave followers, all of whom were more or less wounded. On hearing the cheer, some of the Portugals came towards them with threatening gestures, one of them exclaiming, in tolerably good English—

"You are impudent fellows indeed to cheer when you are miserable prisoners on board the ship of an enemy. Do not you see that we are victorious?"

"Running away is a funny mode of proving it,

Senhor Portugal," answered Dick Lizard, one of the seamen, cocking his eye at the speaker. "If you had cheered, now, we might have thought you had won the day; but I sticks to my opinion that it's we have won the day; and so I say, one cheer more for Old England. Old England forever!"

The Portugal's rage was so great that he would have given Dick a clout on the head which would have finished his shouting, had not Raymond, weak as he was, stepped forward to defend his follower, who was much hurt.

"Shame on you, Senhor Portugal," he exclaimed, standing over Dick with a broken spar which he had grasped to defend him. "What! would you strike a wounded man simply because he shows the satisfaction he feels that our countrymen are free, if not the victors, and not as we are, prisoners?"

"You crow loudly for a cock with his leg tied," said the man, desisting, however, from his attempt to strike poor Dick.

Some more seamen had now assembled, threatening to punish the English for their audacity, when their captain made his appearance among them, inquiring the cause of the disturbance.

"Senhor," he said, turning to Edward, "you are my prisoner, though I wish to treat you as a brave man and a gentleman; but I cannot always restrain my people, who are somewhat lawless in their notions; and I must therefore request that, whatever may be the feelings of your countrymen, they will keep them within bounds."

So many of the Portugals were wounded, that it was some time before the not very skilful surgeons of the ship could attend to the English, who had, and perhaps fortunately for themselves, to doctor their own hurts, which they did, one helping the other in their own rough but efficacious way. It was pleasant to see the hardy tars helping each other like brethren, washing and cleansing each other's wounds — several of them tearing up their shirts to bind up their comrades' limbs, or letting their heads rest with tender care in their laps. Those who had still strength to stand anxiously watched the fast-receding fleet of the English till their loftier masts sank below the horizon, and all hope of being pursued and retaken was abandoned.

"Troth, sir, I suppose, then, we must make the best of a bad job," said Lizard, shrugging his shoulders. "That's my philosophy. I learned it when I was a little chap from my father, who was a great philosopher, seeing that he was a cobbler, and have stuck to it ever since, and never found it fail. What's the odds? says I. Why should a man sigh and groan if he can laugh? why should he cry and moan if he can sing? If things are bad, they can be mended — just as my father used to say of the old shoes brought to him. If that isn't a comfort, I don't know what is."

Most of the Portugal ships escaping from the

fight kept together; but meeting the same hurricane which caused such fearful havoc among the English fleet, they also were separated, some going where so many proud argosies have gone — to the bottom — the Santa Maria, the ship on board which Edward found himself, being left alone to pursue her voyage. Edward suffered much from his wound, and had far from recovered his strength when the Santa Maria arrived at Goa. Goa was at that time the largest European settlement in the East; and here the Portugals, to impress the natives with the beauty of the faith they professed, had established that admirable institution, the benign Inquisition. Here those edifying spectacles, *autos-da-fé*, frequently took place, when men of all ages, women, and even children, were paraded forth, dressed in hideous garments, to be burned alive in consequence of their unwillingness to confess their belief in the doctrines held by the Church. Our chronicle does not decide whether the Portugal priesthood were right or wrong in their proceedings; but, undoubtedly, very few converts were made to the Christian faith, and the influence of their country in the East has long since decreased to zero. The appearance of the place, though deceptive, was in its favor, and innumerable large churches, monasteries, and other public buildings reared their heads on its sandy shores. Those were the days of old Goa's grandeur and magnificence, soon to depart for ever.

Instead, however, of being landed here, the

prisoners were conveyed to the Fort of San Pedro, to the south, lest inconvenient questions might be too often asked as to how they came to be there, and what had become of the rest of the fleet which captured them.

The Castle of San Pedro was a strong fortress with high walls and towers — a gloomy-looking place, as gloomy as any spot in that land of sunshine can be, but gloomy undoubtedly it appeared to poor Edward and his companions, as, strongly guarded, they were conducted through its portals, not knowing when they might repass them and obtain their liberty. They were first conducted into the presence of the governor, a surly old don of the most immovable character; his face was like smoke-dried parchment. with beard of formal cut, and eyes so sunk that nothing could be seen but two small spots of jetty hue, overhung with gray shaggy eyebrows. Without the slightest expression of courtesy or commiseration, he at once commenced interrogating Edward in the Portugal tongue, ordering a yellow-skinned trembling clerk, who squatted at his side with a huge book before him, to write down his replies.

Edward answered succinctly to all the questions put to him, requesting that, as prisoners of war, he and his men might be treated with the courtesy usually awarded to persons in their position, by civilized nations, among whom the Portugals stood prominent.

"Call yourselves prisoners of war!" exclaimed Don Lobo, pulling his mustaches vehemently. "You are pirates — you and your countrymen — nothing better; and as such deserve to be thrown from the top of one of the towers of this castle, or dangled from one of the turrets by a rope, or shot, or drowned — any death is too good for you; burning at the stake as heretics — ay, vile heretics as you are — is most fit for you. See that such is not your lot."

Edward made no reply to this address, feeling that such would only too probably exasperate the petty tyrant. Dick Lizard was, however, not so judicious. Having had a good deal of intercourse with the Portugals, he knew enough of their language to understand what was said; so, putting his left arm akimbo, and doubling his right fist, he exclaimed —

"Call us pirates! I'll tell you what you and your dastardly crew are, Senhor Don Governor: you are a set of garlic-eating, oil-drinking sons of sea-cooks, who rob the weak when you can catch them, and run away from the strong like arrant knaves and cowards as you are. You are" —

What other complimentary remarks poor Dick might have uttered it is impossible to say; for as he was beginning his next sentence, a blow from the but-end of an arquebuse laid him prostrate on the floor. Edward, afraid that his bold countryman had been killed, knelt down by his side. But

Dick's head was too hard to succumb to the strength of a Portugal's arm, even when wielding a heavy weapon.

"All right, sir," he said, opening his eyes. "I'll be at them again, and give 'em more of my mind, and my fist too, if I can get at them."

Edward, however, advised him under the circumstances to keep both one and the other to himself, and, as he did not feel disposed to be polite to his masters, to hold his tongue.

"Masters! Marry, masters, indeed!" cried Dick. "If you says they are masters, sir, I suppose they be; but they'll find me a terrible obstinate servant to deal with, let me tell them."

"No, don't tell them, Lizard, that or any thing else," said Edward soothingly. "You see that at all events we are in their power, and unless they let us go we may have some difficulty in escaping."

"Not if we can get some planks to float on, sir," whispered Lizard. "That notion of yours, sir, has brought me to sooner nor any thing. I thinks as how now, sir, I can keep a civil tongue in my head to those baboon-faced, sneaking, blackguard scoundrels."

"Get up, then, man, and remember not to speak a word while I explain your sentiments," said Edward, glad by any means to save his follower from ill treatment.

The Portugals, who fully believed that the blow

must have inflicted a mortal injury on the man, fancied that his officer was receiving his last dying words, a message to his distant home, and did not interfere with him. Their surprise, therefore, was proportionately great when they saw him get up on his legs, give a hitch to his waistband, and, after sundry scratches and pulls at his shaggy locks, once more address the governor.

"An' may it please your honor, Senhor Don Governor, I axes your reverence's pardon for calling you and your people yellow-faced sons of sea-cooks (because as how to my mind your fathers and mothers were never any thing so respectable," he added in a low tone). "Howsomdever, as your honor knows, I am but a rough seaman who's followed his calling on the salt water all the days of his life, and will follow it, maybe, to the end, and therefore much manners can't be expected; and so, Senhor Scarecrow, or whatever is your name, I hope you'll not log down against my officer here or my shipmates any thing you've heard."

Edward, as soon as he could put in a word, began to offer an interpretation of what had been said. It was not very literal, but interpreters are seldom exact in translation. He remarked that his follower had forgotten himself, that the blow had brought him to his senses, and that he now wished to render every apology in his power to one like Senhor Don Lobo, who so greatly merited his respect.

The old governor pulled away at his beard for some time, and twirled his mustaches, but was at length pacified sufficiently to order the prisoners to be carried off to the ward prepared for them.

Edward, determined to maintain a courteous demeanor in spite of the harshness with which he was treated, bowed to the governor as he was marched off between two guards, who seemed to think that the pugnacious Englishmen would by some means or other break away from them, and effect their escape. For that reason Dick Lizard had no less than six guards, one on each side, and two in front, and two behind; and certainly, as he rolled along with his sea cap stuck on the back of his head, his brawny arms bare, and his broad chest exposed, he appeared capable of successfully accomplishing any design he might conceive on his captors. The rest of the seamen imitated him with more or less effect, and were evidently customers of whom the Portugals stood greatly in awe.

The ward in which the English prisoners were placed was a room in a tower on a third floor overlooking the sea. It might have made a not unpleasant chamber if nicely fitted up, but as the only aperture to admit light and air was strongly barred, as the walls were of rough stone, the floor dirty, and heaps of not the cleanest straw were made to do duty for beds, the state of the case was very different. There were no chairs or tables; so that when the prisoners got tired of walking about they were obliged to betake themselves to their heaps of straw. Here day after day passed by. Edward, however, with the aid of Dick, who firmly believed in his power of escaping, kept up the spirits of the party by inducing them to tell their long and astounding yarns, and singing a variety of songs. Sometimes their guards came in to inquire why they were making so much noise, but they were not generally interfered with. Occasionally they received a visit from the surly old governor, when Edward, instead of asking for better quarters, as he might reasonably have done, treated him with the same respect as at first. Dick Lizard pretended to do the same; but as soon as the stately don had passed him the expression of his features and his gestures showed that his respect was not of an enduring quality. As the governor passed along the ward, Dick would imitate his strut and would give a stately bow, now on one side, now on the other, his countenance all the time in a broad grin. Even the warders and guards were amused by his antics, and for fear of putting a stop to them only gave way to their laughter when they saw that the governor was not looking towards them.

"All right, sir," said Dick to Edward one day, after he had been indulging in more than his usual facetiousness, and the governor had taken his departure. "To my mind these Portugals care very little for their old don, or they wouldn't laugh at him as they do; and it's my belief that we shall be able to bribe them to let us slip out one of these fine nights without making any noise about it, and when the morning comes we shall be gone."

Edward's heart beat with joy at the thought, but after reflecting a little he answered, with a sigh—

"A bright idea, Dick, but I fear me much the wherewithal to bribe is sadly wanting. The rogues have left us little else but the clothes on our backs."

The seaman gave a well-satisfied hitch to his waistband — a movement indicative of satisfaction or hesitation, as well as other emotions of the mind, among nautical characters in all ages — and observed—

"The dons are not quite as clever as they think, sir. They left us our clothes, but I and two more of us had lined them pretty thickly with good lots of yellow-boys, and there they are all safe. You know, sir, a seaman never knows what may happen, and to my mind it's a wise custom among some of us. To be sure, if we comed to be cast away on a desolate island, all the gold in the world wouldn't help a man to get off so much as a sharp axe and a chest of carpenter's tools; but among people with manners and customs, though I can't say much for either one or the other of those hereabouts, there's nothing like gold!"

"True indeed, Lizard," said Edward, partaking somewhat of the confidence of his follower, at the same time that he saw more clearly, probably, the difficulties in their way. He therefore entreated

Dick and the rest to act with the greatest circumspection, and to appear to submit with perfect readiness to the rules and regulations of the place. The good effect of this conduct was apparent by the greater liberty which the prisoners obtained, and they were now allowed to take their exercise in the open air on the flat roof of part of the castle. Thence in a short time they were allowed to descend to a terrace overlooking the sea, where, however, they were watched by several lynx-eyed guards stationed above them.

It is seldom that those shores are visited by storms, but when the wind does blow it makes ample amends for its usual state of quiescence. In spite of a gale which had sprung up, Edward, with Dick Lizard and several of the other prisoners, was walking up and down on the said terrace, when Dick, whose eyes were of the sharpest, exclaimed that he saw a tall ship driving on before the gale, which set directly on the coast.

"Alas for the hapless crew!" exclaimed Edward. "I fear me they will all be lost!"

"Not a doubt about it, sir, unless some truehearted seamen venture out to their rescue when the ship strikes, as strike she must before many hours are over."

"Are you ready to go, Lizard?" asked Edward.

"An' that I am, sir, and all the rest of us, I'll warrant, if a boat can be found to swim in such a sea," answered Dick.

"Then I'll lead you, my brave lads!" said Edward warmly. "I'll go seek the governor and get from him a boat fit for our purpose. Whoever they are, I could not bear to see our fellow-creatures perish without an effort to save them. But perhaps the Portugals themselves will be eager to go, and not thank us for making the offer."

"Not a bit of it," answered Dick sturdily. "I've seen brave Portugals, I'll allow, but when they come out to this country all the good gets burnt out of them."

Dick was not far from right. Edward got access to the governor, who at once inquired if any one was ready to volunteer to go to the rescue of the crew of the ship now closely approaching the land; but when it was understood that the English prisoners had offered to risk their lives in the undertaking, no one was found willing to deprive them of the honor.

A fine seaworthy boat was placed at Edward's disposal, and at the head of his men, who were in the highest spirits, he walked out once more from prison.

Of what nation was the approaching ship was the question. To the honest tars and the brave gentlemen they followed it mattered nothing whether she was friend or foe. The Portugals had, however, discovered her to belong to their own people, and this, although it did not make them the more disposed to risk their own lives, induced them the more willingly to allow the English to do so to any extent they might see fit. Great was the eagerness they exhibited in bringing oars, and tholes, and boathooks, and ropes down to the boat, and still more, when the English had got into her, in launching her into deep water. This could not have been done on the open beach, on which the sea broke with terrific force, but she was hauled up on the shore of a natural harbor formed by two ledges of rocks rising a considerable height above the water. As the outer ends circled round and overlapped each other, the water inside the basin thus formed was comparatively smooth. Outside, however, the sea broke with terrific fury, threatening to overwhelm any boat or other floating machine which might get within its influence.

Some way to the north was another wide extending ledge of rocks, towards which it appeared that the unfortunate ship was drifting; but even should she escape that particular ledge and drive on the beach, the chance that any of those on board would escape was small indeed, for so high were the rollers and so powerful the reflux that once within their influence the stoutest ship could not hold together many minutes, and should any living beings washed towards the shore escape being dashed to pieces or killed by the broken planks and spars, they would be carried again out to sea and lost. Edward and Dick Lizard saw clearly this state of things, but they were not in consequence deterred from attempting to perform their errand of mercy. They also saw that if they would be successful there must be no delay. Each man having secured his oar with a rope, and himself to his seat by the same means, Edward gave the sign to the Portugals to shove off the boat. With loud shouts they placed their shoulders under her sides, and then, shrieking and grunting in concert, they almost lifted her along the sand till she floated, when the English prisoners bringing their oars into play shoved her off into the middle of the basin. Dick Lizard took the helm, while Edward stood up to judge of the best moment for crossing through the breakers. The crew went steadily to their work. No one was ignorant of the danger to be gone through. At the entrance of the little harbor a white wall of water rose up before them, curling round and topped with masses of glittering foam, which fell in dense showers, blown by the gale over them, tending to blind and bewilder even the most experienced seaman of the party. Edward was at first in despair of finding a channel through which the boat could by any possibility pass and live. Some of the Portugals had, however, assured him that at times between the intervals of the heavier seas he would be able to get through, and he resolved to persevere if his men were ready to do so.

"Ready, ay, ready, every one of us, Master Raymond," answered Dick Lizard, after the briefest of consultations with his comrades. "Where's the odds? We can but die once, whether with a Portugal's bullet through us, or by the *vomito prèito*, or under yonder foaming seas — what matters it? An' you wish to go, we, to a man, will go too."

"Thanks, my brave lads; and now, when I order you to give way, give way you must, or be ready to back water at the word," exclaimed Edward, standing up in the stern-sheets of the boat so as to command a view over the mass of seething, raging, roaring water which rose before him. Sea after sea rolled in, and with a voice of thunder broke on the rocks with a force sufficient, it seemed, to dash them to fragments; but, placed there by the hand of Omnipotence to curb the fury of the wild ocean, the proud waters were hurled back upon themselves again and again, unable to gain a foot on their fixed confines, shattered into minute atoms of foam which the wind bore far away on its fleet wings, while the iron rocks remained fixed as of old, laughing to scorn their reiterated attacks.

The ship meantime was approaching nearer and nearer to the shore. Had she been drifting directly on it, she would by that time have been cast helpless on the stern rocks, but happily part of her foremast was still standing, on which a sail being set, her course was somewhat diagonal, and she was therefore longer in reaching her impending fate than had at first appeared likely to be the case. Now she rose on the summit of a foaming sea, now she sank into the hollow, seemingly as if never to appear again; but bravely she struggled on, like a being endued with life, resolved to battle to the last, yet knowing that destruction was inevitable. Edward observed that although at first there appeared to be no difference in the height of the rollers, yet that after a time several of less apparent strength came tumbling in unbroken till they actually touched the rocks, leaving a narrow yet clear space between them. Through this space he determined to urge his boat. He pulled down to the very mouth of the harbor; the crew lay on their oars. A huge sea came roaring on majestically, and breaking into foam almost overwhelmed the boat. Directly afterwards the clear channel appeared.

"Give way, give way, brave lads!" shouted Edward.

The boat sprang on. Immediate destruction or success awaited them. The blades of the oars were concealed amid the seething waters on either side, and the foam came bubbling up over the gunwales, but the boat still held her course outward. She rose towards the summit of a lofty sea; the men strained every nerve. Up she climbed; then downward she slid rapidly to meet another sea, up which she worked her way as before. Another and another appeared in rapid succession; she surmounted them all, and the open ocean was gained.

Having gained a sufficient distance from the land, they had to keep along shore with the sea stream —

a dangerous position, as, should the boat be caught by a roller, she would most certainly be turned over and over till she was dashed in fragments on the beach. On they came to the ship, plunging through the seas, and appearing as if every instant would be her last, even before she could reach the fatal strand. As they drew near they could distinguish the people on board in various attitudes indicative of despair. There were many hapless beings — sailors, soldiers, civilians, and women and children, some infants in arms, all full of life, and yet, ere many fleeting minutes could pass away, to be numbered with the dead. One last desperate effort was, it was seen, now made by the crew of the ship to save their lives. Two anchors were let go, the cables flying out like lightning from the bows, while at the same moment gleaming axes cut away the remaining part of the foremast, which plunged free of the ship into the sea. It was a well-executed, seamanlike manœuvre. The stout ship was brought up, and although she plunged with her lofty bow almost under the seas, it seemed that her anchors were about to hold her. Hope revived in the breasts of those on board. Edward and his brave companions pulled alongside; ropes were hove to them, and they maintained the position they had gained, although in the greatest possible peril of being swamped. To climb up to the deck of the ship was almost impossible, but Raymond shouted out that he was ready to convey as many of the passengers to the shore as were willing to trust themselves to his charge. Many of those who but a short time before had given way to despair were now unwilling to leave the stout ship which still floated under them for a small open boat. Some who had less confidence in the power of the anchors to hold the ship, hurried to the side, and showed by their gestures that they wished to enter the boat. Without assistance, however, to make the attempt were madness, and the Portugal seamen exhibited no intention of helping them.

"I'll do it, Master Raymond," cried Dick Lizard, seizing a rope which hung over the side, and with a nimbleness which alone prevented him from being crushed between the boat and the ship he climbed up over her bulwarks. Two seamen followed his example.

Several more persons came crowding to the side of the vessel on seeing the hardihood of the British seamen in venturing to their assistance. Dick seized the person he found nearest to him as he leaped on deck. It was a young girl. She was clasping the arm of a gray-headed, tall old man, who seemed to be her father.

"No time for ceremony, fair lady," cried Dick; "bless your sweet face, I'll make all square when we gets you safe on shore; just now, do you see, you mustn't mind a little rough handling. There! there! let go the old gentleman's fist; we'll lower him after you, never fear. Hold on taut by the rope, as you love me. A drop of tar won't hurt your pretty hands. There! there! away you go! Look out below there! Gingerly, lads, lower away. Now, old gentleman, you follows your daughter, I suppose?"

These exclamations were all uttered while Dick and his companions were securing a rope round the young lady's waist, and lowering her into the boat. She gazed upward at her father with a look of affection as she felt herself hanging over the raging ocean while the boat seemed receding from her. A loud shriek of terror escaped her. Dick waited till the boat had again risen, and just as it was about to descend into the trough, he let the young girl drop into the arms of Raymond, who stood ready to receive her, and with a sharp knife cut the rope above her head, not waiting to cast it loose. The next comer was, as Dick promised, the old gentleman, who, even less able to help himself than the young lady, was treated much in the same way.

A young mother with her child, whom with one arm she clutched convulsively to her bosom, while with the other with a parent's loving instinct she endeavored to prevent the infant from being dashed against the ship's side, was next lowered. Not a sound did she utter. Once the ship gave an unexpected roll, and she was thrown rudely against the side, but she only clasped her infant the tighter, and heeded not the cruel blows she was receiving. Barely could Edward with all his strength secure her and free her from the rope before the boat was dashed off to a distance from the ship. Again, however, the boat was hauled up alongside. Lizard had now slung two little boys together. Though pale with terror, they bravely encouraged each other as they hung over the foaming ocean till the position of the boat enabled them to be lowered into her.

Their father stood on the bulwarks watching them with all a father's affection, he himself wishing to follow immediately, but being prohibited from making the attempt till some more women and children had been lowered. Lizard and his companions labored on unceasingly, for none of the Portugal's crew would render them any assistance. Several other people were thus conveyed to the boat, but many who seemed at first inclined to leave the ship lost courage as they saw the hazard of the undertaking. Some, again, as they gazed towards the foam-covered shore, and heard the roar of the seas as they dashed on the wild rocks, or rolled up on the shingly beach, showed that they would rather trust their safety to the boat than to the laboring ship. Among them was a young man who pushed forward requesting to be lowered.

"No, no, senhor don," said Lizard. "Do ye see that there are more women and children to go first? We must look after the weaker ones, who can't help themselves. That's the rule we rovers of the ocean stick to."

The young man, either not comprehending him,

or so eager to escape as to forget all other considerations, sprang up on the bulwarks, and, seizing a rope, attempted to lower himself without assistance. Miscalculating the time, he descended rapidly; the ship gave a sudden lurch, the boat swung off, and the foaming sea surging up tore him from the rope, and with a fearful cry of despair he sank for ever. He was the first victim claimed by the ocean. His fate deterred others from making a like attempt.

"Come, senhor," said Lizard to the father of the little boys, "if you wish to go with us it's fair you should, seeing that others are thinking about the matter instead of acting. You just trust to me, and I'll land you safely."

Comprehending what Lizard meant by his gestures, rather than by his words, he submitted himself to his guidance, and was placed by the side of his boys. At that instant a cry arose on board the ship that the anchors were dragging. Lizard soon saw that the report was too true. Now numbers were eager to jump into the boat. She might have carried three more persons, but in the attempt to receive them scores might have leaped in, and the boat would have been swamped. Dick and his companions had no fancy to be wrecked with the ship; so, seizing ropes, they swung themselves into the boat. The next moment the rope which held the boat was cut, and she floated clear of the ship. The oars were got out and hastily plied by the sturdy seamen. Good reason had they to exert all

their strength, for the ship, while dragging her
anchors, had already carried them fearfully near
the roaring line of breakers among which she herself was about to be ingulfed. With horror those
who had been rescued contemplated the impending
fate of their late companions. Slowly the boat
worked her way out to sea, while the ship, with far
greater rapidity, drove towards the shore. Now the
wind, which appeared for an instant to have lulled,
breezed up again. Hardly could the boat hold her
own. Edward and Lizard had to keep their eyes
seaward to watch the waves in order to steer their
boat amid their foaming crests. The hapless people
on board too well knew what must be their own fate.
In vain they shrieked for help; in vain they held
out their arms; vain, truly, was the help of man.
A furious blast swept over the ocean. A mass of
foam broke over the boat. Raymond believed that
she could not rise to the coming sea, but, buoyantly
as before, she climbed up its watery side, struggling
bravely. As she reached its summit a cry escaped
the rowers — "The anchors have parted! Good
God! the anchors have parted!"

In an instant more the raging seas, foaming and
hissing, broke over the stout ship, ingulfing in their
eager embrace many of those who were till then
standing on the deck full of life and strength. Still
the waters seemed to cry out for more. Each time
they rushed up more and more were torn from their
hold. Some strong swimmers struggled for a few

moments amid the boiling surges for dear life, but the shrieks of most of them were speedily silenced in death. The stout ship, too, stout as she was, quickly yielded to the fury of the breakers. The high poop was torn away as if made of thin pasteboard; the wide forecastle, with the remainder of the crew still clinging to it, was carried off and speedily dashed to fragments; the stout hull next, with a wild crash, was rent asunder, and huge timbers, and beams, and planks were dashed to and fro amid the foaming billows, speedily silencing the agonized shrieks of those who yet hoped — though hoped in vain — to reach the land where hundreds upon hundreds of their fellow-creatures stood bewailing their fate, but unable to render them assistance. But a few minutes had passed by since the tall ship had struck on those cruel rocks, and now her shattered fragments strewed the ocean, some carried back by the receding waves, others cast, torn and splintered, on the beach with tangled masses of ropes, and spars, and seaweed. Here and there a human form, mangled, pallid, and lifeless, could be discerned, surrounded by the remnants of the wreck, now approaching, now again dashed off suddenly from the shore; now an arm might be seen lifted up as if imploringly for help; now the head, now the very lips, might be seen to move, but it was but the dead mocking at the living. No sound escaped those lips; for ever they were to be silent. Most of those thus momentarily seen were swept off again to become the prey of the ravenous monsters of the deep. A few of the poor remnants of frail mortality were cast up and left upon the shore, whence they were carried up by the pitying hands of charity to be interred in their mother earth, but by far the greater number were among those who shall rest in their ocean graves till the time arrives when the sea shall give up her dead, and all, from every land and every clime throughout all ages since the world was peopled, shall meet together for judgment.

CHAPTER VI.

"How fares it with the good ship, Dick?" asked Edward, fearing for one moment to withdraw his eyes from off his arduous task of steering the boat amid the raging seas.

The answer came not from the British seaman, but from one of the passengers taken from the ship:—

"Mother of Heaven! they are lost — all lost!"

The words, uttered by the young lady who had been the first received into the boat, were followed by a heart-rending shriek as she sank fainting into the arms of her father. Many of those who had been saved had relatives, all had friends and acquaintances, on board the ship. Some others cried out and expressed their horror or regret, but the greater number looked on with stolid indifference, satisfied that they had themselves escaped immediate destruction, or absorbed in the selfish contemplation of their own pending fate. It seemed even now scarcely possible that the boat, heavily laden as she was, could escape being swamped. Humanly speaking, her safety depended on the bone and muscle and perseverance of her crew. None but true British seamen could have held out as they did. Many hours had elapsed since the ship was first seen; night was approaching, and the sea still ran so high that it would be next to madness to attempt re-entering the little harbor — a task far more difficult than getting out of it, as the slightest deviation to the right or left would have caused the instant destruction of the boat and of all on board her. There was nothing, therefore, but to continue at sea. There was no other harbor for many miles either to the north or south which they could hope to reach within many days.

"An' we had but provender aboard, Master Raymond, we might give the Portugals the slip, and never let them see our handsome faces again," observed Dick, after keeping silence for a considerable time.

"True, Dick," answered Edward, and hope rose in his heart at the bare mention of escaping; but with a sigh he added, "First, though, we have no provender, and had we, in duty we are bound to land these poor people as soon as we can with safety venture so to do. Already they are almost worn out, and a few hours more of exposure may destroy their lives, which we have undergone this peril to preserve. Then, again, the Portugals allowed us to take the boat on the faith that we were to return. Duty is duty, Dick; the temptations to neglect it do not alter its nature, whatever the old tempter Satan may say to the contrary. Let us stick to duty and never mind the consequences."

"That's all true, no doubt, Master Raymond, what you say," replied Lizard. "But it would be hard, if there was a chance of getting away, to go back to prison. Liberty is sweet, especially to seamen."

"Duty is duty, Dick," repeated Raymond. "What is right is the right thing to do ever since the world began. Maybe the gale will go down, and by dawn we may land these poor people without danger. It will be a happy thing to us to have saved them; and, to my mind, even our prison will be less dreary from having done it."

All hands were soon brought round to their officer's opinion. The sun was now setting, and darkness in that latitude comes on immediately afterwards. Their prospect was therefore dreary and trying in the extreme. It was difficult to keep the boat free from water in the day; still more difficult would it be while night shrouded the ocean with her sombre mantle. Hunger, too, was assailing the insides of the crew; but, still undaunted, they prepared to combat with all their difficulties. Rest they must not expect; their safety depended on their pulling away without ceasing at the oars. Pull they did right manfully. Now one broke into a song; now another cheered the hearts of his companions with a stave, which he trolled forth at the top of his voice. The example was infectious, and in spite of hunger and fatigue, jokes and laughter and songs succeeded each other in rapid succession.

The jokes were none of the most refined, nor were the songs replete with wisdom; but the laughter, at all events, was loud and hearty; above all things, it had the effect of raising the drooping spirits of the poor beings who had been confided to them by Providence.

As they sang, and joked, and rowed, the sea began to go down, and thus, as their strength decreased, the necessity of exerting it became less; still they were compelled to pull on to keep the boat off the land and her head to the sea. At length the singers' voices grew lower and lower, and the jokers ceased their jokes, and the heads of some as they rowed dropped on their bosoms for an instant, but were speedily raised again with a jerk and a shake as they strove to arouse their faculties. Edward had need of all his energies to keep himself to his task, and he told Dick to warn him should he show any signs of drowsiness.

The hours as the morning approached appeared doubly long. The dawn came at last, and then the sun in a blaze of glory shot upward through the sky and cast his burning rays across the waters upon the boat, with her living but almost exhausted freight yet struggling bravely. The wind had fallen. There was a perfect calm, but yet the billows rolled on, moved, it seemed, by some mysterious power unseen to human eye — not, as before, broken and foaming, but in long, smooth, glassy rollers. Smooth as they were, they would have proved fatally treacherous to thé boat had Raymond ventured to land. As they approached the beach they gained strength and height, and then broke with tremendous fury on the smooth sand or rugged rocks, as if indignant at being stayed in their course. Again and again Edward and his companions gazed wistfully at the coast. That formidable line of breakers still prohibited approach. He and his companions had before been suffering from hunger. As the sun rose higher and became hotter and hotter, thirst assailed them — thirst more terrible and more fatal than hunger. The poor passengers suffered most;. it seemed as if they had escaped a speedy death on the previous day, to suffer one more painful and lingering. Raymond had been unable till now to pay them much attention personally, leaving them to assist each other as best they could. He was now attracted by the affectionate manner in which the young lady who had been at first saved tended her aged father, and at length, when he could with safety leave the helm, on stooping down to aid her, he recognized in her features, careworn as they were, those of Donna Isabel d'Almeida. He addressed her by name.

"What! then our gallant deliverer is the Englishman Don Edoardo, the friend of Don Antonio!" she exclaimed. "Father, father, we are safe among friends; they will surely take us to the shore when they can. I perceived the likeness from the first, but, overcome with terror and confusion, I could not assure myself of the fact. You will forgive me, Don Edoardo."

"Indeed, fair lady, I have nothing to forgive," said Edward. "I rejoice to have been the means of thus far preserving one for whom I have so high an esteem from a dreadful fate. I cannot but believe that Providence, which has saved us thus far, will enable us yet to reach the shore in safety."

"Heaven and all the saints grant that we may! and under your guidance I have no fear," answered Donna Isabel. "But, Don Edoardo"—

The young lady stopped and hesitated, and then continued in a faint voice—

"There was another brave officer of your ship I would ask after—Don Antonio. I could never pronounce his family name. How is it that he is not with you?"

This question very naturally led Edward to describe the battle, and how he had been taken prisoner and brought to Goa, and thence transferred to the safe keeping of Don Lobo, and how he and his companions had been treated, and how they had been enabled to come off to the assistance of the ship in consequence of the cowardice of her countrymen, who were glad to get others to do the work which they were afraid to attempt.

This account was listened to with interest by the rest of the passengers, who all exclaimed against the cruelty and injustice of Don Lobo, and promised, should they be preserved, to use their influence in obtaining the liberty of the brave Englishmen.

"See, Dick, did I not say right when I told thee that we should do our duty, and leave the consequences to Providence?" Raymond could not help remarking to Lizard. "We shall now have many friends about us on shore, and some of them will get us set free, depend on that."

"I hope you are right, Master Raymond; but to my mind the Portugal chaps haven't much gratitude in their nature, and out of sight with them is out of mind," was Dick's reply.

As the day drew on, the anxiety of all in the boat to reach the land increased; indeed, it was very evident that without water several would be unable to exist through another night. Accordingly, about four hours after noon, as was guessed by the height of the sun, Raymond announced his intention of making the attempt to run into the harbor. He had carefully noted the bearings of the marks at the entrance on coming out, so that he was able to steer a direct course for the spot. The long swells still rolled in, and broke along the coast in sheets of foam, and all he hoped to find were a few yards of green water through which he might steer his boat. The belief that their toils were to come to an end roused up even the most exhausted of the crew. On glided the boat. Now those on board looked down on the shore full in view before them — now a smooth green wall of water rose up and shut it from their sight. Even the bravest held their breath as they approached the rocks, and the loud roar of the breakers sounded in their ears. Edward and Lizard stood up, grasping the tiller between them. There was no going back now. Had they allowed the boat to come broadside to one of those watery heights she would instantly have been rolled over and over, and cast helpless on the rocks. Many a silent prayer was offered up that such a fate might be averted. Nearer and nearer the boat approached the rocks. "Back water — back water, lads!" cried Raymond, and a huge roller lifted the boat high above the shore, but failed to carry her forward. It broke with a thundering roar into sheets of foam, and then opened before them a smooth channel. "Pull — pull for your lives, lads!" cried Edward. The seamen obeyed with a will. The boat shot on, and, amid showers of spray on either hand, ere a breath could be completely drawn, she was gliding forward, all dangers passed, towards the beach, where hundreds of persons, Portugals and natives, stood ready to receive them. The boat was hauled up on the beach, and, this task accomplished, even Edward and Lizard sank down, unable to support themselves. They and their companions were carried up to the castle, and, although somewhat better chambers were provided for them, they found themselves still prisoners, and strictly guarded.

"I told you so, Master Raymond — I told you

so!" exclaimed Dick. "There's no gratitude in these Portugals."

However, after the lapse of a few days their condition was altered very much for the better, and provisions and luxuries of various sorts were sent in as presents from those who had heard of their brave exploit. Raymond also received visits from Don Joao d'Almeida, as also from various other persons of influence. He was himself allowed rather more liberty than before, and was even permitted to ride out in a morning with an escort, in company with some of the officers of the fort, and to enter into such society as the place afforded. He thus constantly met the young Donna Isabel, whom he could not help regarding with interest. At the same time, whatever might have been his private opinion regarding the attractions of that fair lady, even had they been far greater than he esteemed them, he would not have allowed himself to be influenced by them; first because there was one in his far-off home to whom his troth was plighted, and secondly because he fancied that her affections were fixed on Waymouth, and though he devoutly hoped that his friend would never marry her, yet he considered that as a messmate and a friend he was not the person to stand between them. These were the very reasons which suggested themselves to his mind as an excuse, as it were, for not following the rules of all romances, and falling desperately in love with the young lady whom he had been the means of preserving from a dreadful death.

It is possible that even had Edward not been influenced by these two reasons for not falling in love, as the phrase goes, with Donna Isabel, he might have found others — indeed, that she was a Romanist and of a different nation would have had great power with him alone — but it is not necessary to enter into them; the fact remains, he did not in the slightest degree set his affections on her. He, however, believing firmly that she was in love with Waymouth, and having a true and honest heart himself, placing full confidence in the constancy of woman, undoubtedly paid her great attention — such courteous attention as a brother would pay a sister, or an honest man his friend's wife, certainly thinking no evil, or that evil could arise therefrom.

Now it happened that Don Lobo, the governor of the Castle of San Pedro and its dependencies, was a bachelor, and, although a surly, cruel, and morose fellow, had a heart susceptible of the tender passion, or rather of what he fancied was the tender passion, for it would be difficult to suppose any thing tender connected with him. It had been very long since he had seen anybody so young and so beautiful as Donna Isabel, and no sooner did he set eyes on her after she had recovered from the effects of her voyage and exposure in the open boat than he began to be unusually agitated, nor could he rest night or day for thinking of her. His siestas in his hammock at noon, with slaves fanning his face, brought him no rest, nor was it afforded by his couch at night. He resolved to make Donna Isabel his wife. He did all he could to exhibit his feelings towards her; but, powerful as they might have been, and although she might have discovered what they were, she certainly did not return them.

Notwithstanding this, matters went on smoothly enough for some time. Don Lobo was not a despairing lover, and he knew enough of the female sex to be aware that their feelings are not altogether immutable, even if they change only by slow degrees. Donna Isabel's sentiments might alter, and he might reach a high point in her favor. Time, however, passed on as it has done ever since the world began, and no such change as the governor anticipated took place; on the contrary, as the young lady's eyes were more and more opened to the true state of the case, so did her dislike to the don the more and more increase. Indeed, whenever she looked at him, or thought about him, or heard him spoken of, it was with a feeling rather akin to disgust than to devotion. She did not, nevertheless, exhibit these uncomplimentary sentiments as forcibly as under other circumstances she might have done. She and her father were, in the first place, guests of Don Lobo, and dependent on him. Poor Don Joao had also lost all his property in the ship, and, it having been supposed that he was lost, another person had been appointed to his proposed government, and he had to wait till he could receive a fresh appointment from home. Don Lobo was also rich, and had pressed money on Don Joao, which he had accepted, and had thus become still more indebted to him. All these circumstances would have made it very impolitic in Donna Isabel to exhibit her real sentiments, which she was thus in part compelled to disguise, though she could not do so altogether; nor did she afford the slightest encouragement to her unattractive admirer. At first the surly don was very indifferent to this state of things.

"She'll yield — she'll yield before long to my powerful persuasions and personal attractions," he observed to his confidant and factotum, Pedro Pacheco, a worthy always ready to do his master's behests, whatever they might be. "I'll put on my new doublet and hose, and my jewel-hilted sword, and I'll attack her again this day manfully."

"Certainly, most certainly, Senhor Don Lobo. A man of your excellency's superlative qualities, no female heart, however hard, can possibly long withstand," observed Pedro.

"I knew that would be your opinion, my faithful Pedro," said the governor — the fact being that the faithful Pedro always did agree with his patron, not troubling himself to decide whether he thought him right or wrong. In this instance both were wrong.

The governor, to the surprise of the garrison, who had been always accustomed to see him wearing a greasy old doublet and a rusty-hilted sword, made his appearance in a richly ornamented suit, which, though somewhat fusty from having been long shut up, had the advantage of being costly.

He was received, however, as usual by Donna Isabel, who, though she could not help remarking that he wore a handsomer dress than usual, said nothing whatever which might lead him to suppose that she saw in him the least improvement. He tried to talk, but in vain; not a word of sense could he produce. Then he tried to look unutterable things, but he only grinned and squinted horribly, till he frightened the young lady out of her senses, and made her suppose that he was thoroughly bent on going into a fit. Although he did not suspect the cause, he had the wit to discover that he had not made a favorable impression, and returned to his quarters disappointed and not a little angry with his ill success. Pedro Pacheco could only advise him to try again. He might have acted a more friendly part if he had said "Give it up." Don Lobo did try again, and with the like ill success.

"Persevere," said Pedro.

The governor did persevere day after day, and at length, in spite of the entire absence of all encouragement, declared his passion. Donna Isabel frankly told him that she did not love him, and did not believe that she ever should. She might have said she did not think she ever could. He said nothing, but made his bow and exit. He told Pedro Pacheco of his ill fortune.

"Then she loves another!" observed Pedro.

"Who can he be?" exclaimed the governor in a fierce voice.

"Where have your excellency's eyes been of late?" asked the confidant quietly.

"What!" cried Don Lobo, giving a furious pull at his beard, "that Englishman?"

"The same," said Pedro Pacheco, nodding his head.

"Then I will take good care he no longer interferes with me," said the don in a savage tone.

"Of course it would be unwise not to exert your authority when you have him in your power," said Pedro. "Better put him out of the way altogether."

"He has friends — I must have an excuse," said the governor.

"He has been plotting or will be plotting to make his escape," observed Pedro. "To effect this he would not scruple to murder all in the castle. He and his companions have shown what daring rogues they are by going out to the rescue of Donna Isabel and the rest when none of our heroic countrymen would attempt the exploit. Ah, those English are terrible fellows!"

"Proof must be brought to me of their abominable intentions, and then we shall have this officer and his men in our power," observed the governor savagely.

"Proof, your excellency! there will be no want of that, considering that our garrison consists of the very scum of the streets of Lisbon," answered the confidant. "Why, we have men here who for a peço have sworn away the lives of their most intimate acquaintances. Of course, in so admirable a cause they would have no scruple in swearing whatever we may dictate, even should it not be absolutely correct."

"What you may dictate, honest Pacheco, not we, understand," said the governor. "They may bungle when brought into court as witnesses, and though under ordinary circumstances that would not matter, some of these shipwrecked persons are likely to be favorable to them, and might report unfavorably of me if matters did not go smoothly. As to the means I am indifferent when so important a result is to be attained."

"Ah, most noble governor, I understand all about your wishes in the matter, and will take care that the affair is carried out in a satisfactory way," answered the honest Pedro, making his master an obsequious bow as he left the room.

Don Lobo clinched his fist, and, grinding his teeth, struck out as if he had got his prisoner's face directly in front of him. The performance of this act seemed to afford him infinite satisfaction, for he walked up and down the room with a grin which might in courtesy have been called a smile on his countenance for some time till his legs grew weary of the exercise.

Not long after this, Edward was one evening

pacing the terrace facing the sea, casting many a longing glance over the glass-like water of the ocean, on which the rays of the setting sun had spread a sheet of golden hue, and he was considering by what means he could possibly with his companions make his escape, when rough hands were laid on his shoulders and he found his arms suddenly pinioned from behind. His first impulse was to endeavor to shake them off, and having by a violent effort done so, his next was to double his fists and to strike at them right and left, knocking two of them down at the instant in a true British fashion. At that instant, Dick Lizard, coming on the terrace and seeing his officer assailed, rushed forward to his assistance, and quickly sent two more Portugals tumbling head over heels right and left of him.

"To the rescue! to the rescue!" he shouted out, and his voice quickly collected all the English prisoners who were within hearing. Of course more Portugals hurried up to the spot, who at once joined in the fray. Swords and daggers were drawn, which the Englishmen quickly wrenched from the hands of their assailants, though not till several of the prisoners had been wounded; and now the clash of steel was heard and fire-arms were discharged, and the skirmish became general. In the midst of it Pedro Pacheco rushed out of his quarters, crying out —

"Treason! treason! the English are rising and

murdering every one of us," and at the same moment he levelled a pistol at Raymond's head. The bullet would probably have ended the life of the gallant adventurer had not Dick Lizard struck up the Portugal's arm, for he had no time in the first instance to do more, but a second blow from his fist sent Senhor Pedro sprawling on the ground among several others of his party who had been placed in the same horizontal position by the sturdy Englishmen.

In spite of the superior numbers of the Portugals, the fate of so many of their party made the rest unwilling to close with the prisoners, who, not knowing what was intended, stood boldly at bay, resolved to sell their lives dearly, Dick Lizard singing out—

"Come on — come on, ye varlets! we don't fear ye. One Spaniard lick two Portugee, one Englishman lick all three!"

This state of things could not, however, last long. Trumpets were sounding, drums were beating, and soldiers from all quarters were collecting, who now with Don Lobo at their head surrounded the Englishmen. At the command of the governor they were levelling their matchlocks (fortunately the matter of discharging them was not a speedy operation), when Don Joao d'Almeida and his daughter Donna Isabel made their appearance on the scene with most of those who had been preserved from the wreck.

"Hold, hold, countrymen!" cried Don Joao. "What! are you about to slaughter those who so gallantly risked their lives to save ours? Hold, I say; I am sure that you, Don Edoardo, have done nothing intentionally to deserve this treatment."

Donna Isabel joined her entreaties with those of her father.

"Certainly I have no wish to break the peace," answered Raymond. "The arms we hold were taken from those who assailed us, and we are ready to lay them down instantly at the command of the governor, in whose lawful custody we consider ourselves."

Thus appealed to, Don Lobo could not, without outraging all law, order the destruction of his prisoners. Those who had possessed themselves of weapons put them down, when they were immediately seized each by not less than six Portugals, and marched off to the cells in which they had at first been confined.

"I must inquire into the cause of this outbreak, when punishment will be awarded to the guilty," said Don Lobo, as he stalked back to his quarters.

The unpleasant look which the governor cast on him made Edward feel that evil was intended. His suspicions were speedily confirmed, for instead of being taken to the chamber he had lately occupied, he was marched off to the prison in which he and his companions had at first been confined, and was thrust alone into a dark, close, foul dungeon, at a distance, he feared, from Lizard and his other men. He knew nothing of the jealous feelings which had sprung up in the bosom of Don Lobo, or his apprehensions would naturally have been greatly increased. The air of the dungeon was noxious and oppressive, and he had not been in it many hours before he began to feel its ill effects.

"A week or two in such a hole as this will bring my days to a close," he said to himself as he surveyed, as far as the obscurity would allow, the narrow confines of his prison-house. "Alas! alas! my adventure has turned out ill indeed. My own Beatrice, for thy sake I left my native land, and thou wilt have, ere long, to mourn me dead. For thy sake, sweet girl, I pray that I may escape."

In this strain he soliloquized for some time, as people in his circumstances are apt to do, and then he set to work to consider how, by his own exertions, he might be able to get free. He was fain to confess, that, unaided, he had not the slightest chance of escape. Of one thing, however, he was certain — that Dick Lizard would not rest day or night till he had made an attempt to help him. And he knew that Dick, with all a sailor's bluntness and thoughtlessness, had a considerable amount of ready wit, and of caution too, where it was necessary for the accomplishment of an important object. Edward hoped also that his friends would prove true, and exert themselves in his favor.

All this time Don Lobo had resolved on his destruction, and only waited the best opportunity of accomplishing it. Knowing the character of the dungeon in which his prisoner was confined, he believed that he should have very little trouble about the matter. Edward's constitution was, however, very sound, and though he certainly suffered in health, he did not break down altogether, as the governor expected would be the case. Don Lobo, therefore, announced publicly that he intended to bring the prisoners engaged in the late outbreak to a trial. This every one knew well would result in their being shot. Day after day passed by. Edward found his imprisonment more and more irksome, while he had not yet succeeded in communicating with Lizard, nor could he ascertain even where the honest fellow was shut up. His jailers were only conversable when they had any disagreeable news to communicate, and it is extraordinary how loquacious they became when the day of his trial was fixed, and the opinion as to his fate was formed. They seemed to take especial delight in taunting him and in annoying him in every way.

"Ah, senhor, many an honest man has been hung before now, and many a rogue, and neither seems to think it a pleasant operation," remarked one of the fellows, imitating the contortions of countenance of a strangled person.

"To which class does the noble senhor belong, I wonder?" said another.

"Maybe to the last, if he will pardon me saying so," observed a third with a grin.

"But, ah me! rogue or honest, there will be some fair ladies mourning for him in more ports than one," cried another, who was considered the wit of the gang. "Permit me, senhor, to convey your last dying message to some or all of them. Maybe in your own land there is some fair young dame from whom you would not willingly be parted, eh? I thought that I should hit the right nail on the head."

"Peace — peace, men!" exclaimed Edward. "For your own sakes, lest you should ever be in a like condition, allow me to be alone."

His appeal, made with dignity and calmness, had more effect than he expected, and the men shrank back, for a time, at least, abashed. Their last remarks did not, however, affect his feelings as might have been supposed, the fact being that his Beatrice was never out of his thoughts, and night and day his prayers had been for blessings on her head.

The day of the Englishmen's trial approached. Of the result there could not be a shadow of doubt. Numerous witnesses were able to prove that they had been found in open insurrection with arms in their hands, while there was no one to speak in their favor. Any thing, also, like justice was unknown in the land. Still, Don Lobo, having resolved to get rid of his supposed rival, wished to give as great an air of formality and legality to his proceedings as he possibly could.

Edward, from all he could ascertain, felt convinced that he had not many days to live. The night before his trial arrived he had thrown himself on the heap of straw which served as his bed by night and his only seat by day, that he might obtain some repose, the better to go through his ordeal on the morrow, when he heard his prison-door open gently, without the usual creaking noise which announced the appearance of his jailers, and a bright light streamed on his closed eyes. He fancied that he must be dreaming, till he unclosed them and discovered that the light was held by a being habited in a white robe, beautiful in appearance, whether celestial or human he could not at first decide. If the latter, she was young and of the fair sex. He looked again. Yes — Donna Isabel d'Almeida stood before him. She put her finger to her lips to impose silence, and kneeling down by his side whispered for some time into his ears. She then produced a couple of files and other instruments for forcing off shackles, which she and the prisoner plied so assiduously that scarcely half an hour had passed before he stood up free from his chains.

"Take off your shoes and put on these woollen slippers, and follow me, senhor," whispered Donna Isabel. "The guards are asleep, and if no noise is made we need not fear being stopped."

Edward could scarcely believe his senses, and fancied that he must be asleep, but still he wisely did as he was bid. He, however, felt scarcely able to walk after being shut up for so long in that pestiferous dungeon. Donna Isabel, shrouding part of the lantern, glided towards the door, which opening noiselessly she passed out, he following. She led the way up a narrow, dark, winding staircase. It had not many steps, and Edward, to his surprise, found himself pacing a long passage, the end of which he could not distinguish. He had never before been in that part of the fort. Not a sound was heard, nor did his own nor his guide's footfall make the slightest noise. He conjectured that the guard had just before made the rounds, and that the warders had settled themselves into their nooks and corners and gone to sleep. Donna Isabel seemed to have perfect confidence that all was right, though he could not help expecting every instant to come on one of these nooks, and to find a warder prepared to dispute their onward progress.

He had been aware that his dungeon was at a considerable depth, but, judging from the number of steps he had to ascend, he found that it was even deeper down than he had supposed. The gallery was low and arched — hewn out of the rock it appeared, or built of rough stones, though, as may be supposed, he made no very exact observations as he hurried on. Suddenly Donna Isabel stopped, and taking his arm led him round a corner into

10

another corridor or gallery. It was a side passage, or, probably, rather a passage which had been commenced but not finished. Covering up her lantern, they were in total darkness. Edward had, however, time to ascertain that they were behind a buttress or projecting part of the wall, which would conceal them partially from any one passing along the main gallery they had quitted. Donna Isabel had not sought the place of concealment a moment too soon, for scarcely was the light shrouded than footsteps were heard and a glare of light appeared. The light proceeded from a couple of torches held by two men, and directly behind them stalked no less a person than the governor himself, followed closely by Pedro Pacheco. The glare penetrated to the recess in which the fugitives stood, and Edward expected every moment to be discovered by Don Lobo. The don was, however, near-sighted, or so occupied in earnest conversation, that he did not turn his eyes in that direction. Edward could hear his companion's heart beat. Discovery would have been destruction to both of them probably — to him certainly. The governor, also — as was his habit — walked along with his eyes on the ground, but those of the worthy Pedro had the custom of continually casting furtive glances here and there, as if he expected some one to jump suddenly upon him and give him a stab in the ribs or a kick in a less noble part, or as if he thought a person was about to creep behind him to listen to what he was saying.

Edward had remarked this peculiarity in the governor's confidant, and had very natural apprehensions that it would lead to their detection. The eyes went up and down, here and there, as usual — now, by a turn of the head, looking over one shoulder, now over the other, now into the governor's face to ascertain what effect his remarks were producing. Donna Isabel crouched down, really now trembling with fear, for, as far as her gentle nature would allow, she loathed Senhor Pedro even more than his master. Edward stood bolt upright, with his arms by his side and his eyes fixed, to occupy as little space as possible. Round and round went Pedro's lynx-like orbs. By what possibility could they escape falling on the spot where Edward was endeavoring to hide?

A small matter often produces an important result. A little stone, which hundreds of feet had passed by without touching, lay on the ground. The governor struck his toe against it, on which toe a painful callosity existed. Uttering an oath at the pain he was caused, he stumbled forward, and would have proved the hardness of the rock with the tip of his nose had not Pedro caught him as he fell. So assiduous were the attentions of the confidant, that, though Don Lobo limped on slowly, they had both passed beyond the spot from which they could see the fugitives before Pedro's eyes turned again towards the quarter where they stood. It might be possible that other persons were following, but no one else appeared.

It occurred to Edward that the governor might be on his way to see him in his cell, and if so their flight would speedily be discovered. At all events, not a moment was to be lost. Donna Isabel must have thought the same, for, taking his hand, she again led him along the chief gallery in the direction in which they were before going.

"The stumble of the governor might be fortunate for more reasons than one," thought Edward. "If he is going towards my cell, it may delay him and give us a little longer start."

Distances appear much greater to persons walking in the dark and in an unknown path, and thus Edward believed that they must be close on some outlet long before one was reached. More steps were ascended and others descended, and long passages traversed, when Donna Isabel led the way through a narrow one which turned off at right angles to a main gallery, and hurrying along it for some way, they suddenly came to a door. The cool night air came through an iron grating, showing that it was an outlet, if not to the fort itself, to that portion where the prison was placed. Iron bars secured it, and a strong lock, apparently. The lady beckoned to Edward to undertake the task which her weaker arms were unable to perform, throwing the light of the lantern for the purpose on the door. The bolts having been without much difficulty withdrawn, she produced a key, which she handed to Edward. In vain he attempted to fit it in the lock. It was clearly the wrong key, or they had come to the wrong door. There was a latch, but though he pulled at it and shook it, the door would not open.

"Alas! I trust the error is not fatal. We should have turned to the right instead of to the left," whispered Donna Isabel. "It was the only point about which I had any doubt."

Leaving the door with the bolts withdrawn, they retraced their steps for some distance.

"Here! here!" whispered Donna Isabel. "This is the right way."

Going on, they stood before a door similar to the one they had before attempted. The bolts were withdrawn with ease; they had evidently lately been oiled. Passing through the gateway, Edward and the lady found themselves in the open air. Edward expected to be outside the fort, but he soon discovered that they were still within the outer works. The heavy footsteps of a sentry as he paced the ramparts could be distinctly heard, the bark of a dog in the distance, and the steady lash of the restless sea on the beach. A wide open space had to be crossed. The attempt must be made, and yet they might be seen by the sentry. Fortunately the night was dark. Donna Isabel held Edward back till the man had turned, and then whispering, "Quick, quick!" led the way, running rapidly across the open space. So quickly she ran, that Edward could scarcely keep up with her. Breathless she reached the parapet of the outer works. At the spot where they stood an angle sheltered them from the sight of the sentry above. Edward looked over, and found that it was directly above the shore, and, as far as he could judge in the darkness, the ditch seemed to have been almost filled with sand. Donna Isabel, stooping down, produced a strong rope from under a gun-carriage, to which the end was secured.

"I doubt not its strength," she whispered; "but I will lead the way."

And before Edward could prevent her grasping the rope, she had flung herself off the wall, and was descending rapidly. Believing that she had reached the bottom, he imitated her example. The rope stretched and cracked as his weight was thrown on it. Every moment he expected it to break, and he was unable to tell the height he might have to fall, or the nature of the ground which he should reach. It was with inexpressible satisfaction that his feet touched some hard, rugged rocks.

"We have yet farther to go," said Donna Isabel. "Then, Don Edoardo, I must leave you with those better able than a weak girl to render you assistance."

Along the rough sea-beat rocks Donna Isabel, with unfaltering steps, held her way. The softer sand was gained, and now faster even than before she fled along, urging Edward to still greater speed.

"Go before me, brave Englishman," she exclaimed. "Even now we may be pursued, and my failing strength will not bear me on as fast as you can run. On, on; care not for me; I will follow."

This, however, Edward could not bring himself to do. It was contrary to all his manly feelings, his ideas of chivalry. Half lifting and half supporting the young lady, he bore her on towards the harbor. As they went, the idea occurred to him, "What could be Donna Isabel's intentions? Did she propose flying with him?" The question was perplexing. "I'll tell her at once the truth, and return to prison rather than place her in a wrong position."

While thus hurrying on, however, he found it impossible to express his sentiments.

The beach which formed the inner side of the little harbor was at length reached, but no boat could Edward discern.

"It is farther out, concealed under the rocks," said Donna Isabel. "We must endeavor to reach it by walking along them."

The undertaking appeared very hazardous to Edward, who remembered that there were numerous crevices, and smooth, slippery places, down which it would be difficult to avoid falling. Donna Isabel, however, assured him that she was acquainted with a secure path which had been cut in the rocks.

After searching for a short time the path was found, and cautiously she led the way along it. It was necessary in the dark to feel every step in advance, lest a false one might precipitate her into the water. The delay was very trying. Neither of them had once looked behind; there would have been no use in so doing. Even if pursued, they could not have fled faster than they had done. Suddenly Donna Isabel stopped.

"I cannot find the path," she exclaimed, after searching round for some time.

In vain Edward tried to discover it.

While stopping in consequence of this, their eyes were directed for the first time towards the castle. In front of it appeared several bright lights; they were those of torches and lanterns. After flitting about for some time, the lights began to move towards the harbor. They were pursued. If the boat could not be found, they would inevitably be captured.

"I will go first and search for the boat, at all hazards,". exclaimed Edward.

He walked on. Donna Isabel in her alarm had fancied that they were out of the path, though it was but some roughness of the rock that had misled her. They were soon again in it. With renewed spirits Edward pushed on. He fancied that he saw the boat close under a projecting part of the rock. He hailed.

"All right, huzza!" answered a voice. He recognized it as that of Dick Lizard. "We are here, most of us. The Portugals have got three still, but they'll be out soon and come on here."

Dick, being low down, had not seen the lights near the castle. Edward told him of the circumstance.

"Then the poor fellows will be caught," cried Dick. "If we had a chance we'd go back and help them; but we've none. It's the chance of war. If the scoundrel Portugals kill them, we'll avenge them some day. But step in, sir, and we'll shove off. We are sadly short-handed, that's the worst of it, if we are chased. However, it can't be helped."

Edward had not spoken to Donna Isabel for some seconds, or it might be a minute or two; certainly not since he had heard Lizard's voice. Now came the perplexing point, what would she do? Don Joao was not in the boat, nor any of her countrymen. Would she desire to accompany him? He turned to address her, to express his deep gratitude for her noble exertions, and the arrangements she had made thus far so successfully to enable him to escape. Great and painful was his astonishment, however, when, on turning, Donna Isabel was nowhere to be seen. Lizard had not perceived her.

"When I first caught sight of you, Master Raymond, you were alone; that I'll swear, sir," he replied.

Edward sprang back horrified.

"Donna Isabel! Donna Isabel!" he shouted. He felt as grieved and alarmed as he would have done had she been a beloved sister. The dreadful idea seized him that she must have slipped off the rock and been drowned; for calm as was the sea, the swell sent a constant current into the harbor, which would instantly have drawn her away from the spot where she had fallen.

"Donna Isabel! Donna Isabel!" he again shouted.

No answer was given. To delay longer would have been useless. Dick and the other men had joined in the fruitless search. They now literally forced him into the boat, and, shoving off, began to pull down the harbor. As they did so, one of the men declared he saw an object floating by — an uplifted hand. On they pulled; it was ahead. Again it was seen. At that moment lights appeared on the beach, and advancing along the rocks. The fugitives were, however, on the element they loved. They were free. A few strokes more and they would be out of the harbor, when, alas! the stem of the boat struck against a chain drawn tightly across the mouth, and the loud cries and derisive shouts of the Portugals told them that their hopes of escape were vain.

CHAPTER VII.

It would be impossible thoroughly to describe the feelings of disappointment which the Englishmen experienced when they discovered that they were caught like fish in a net. The Portugals were advancing along the rocks on both sides of the harbor, and in the narrow channel where they were they would all be shot down, or must yield directly they were summoned. In vain they tried to break through the chain. Again and again they dashed the stem of their boat against it. No weapon of sufficient strength to cut it was to be found in the boat. Dick and another man leaped overboard, and, balancing themselves on the chain, attempted to lift the boat over, but she was far too heavy to allow them a chance of success. Hitherto the Portugals had not fired; it might have been because they believed that Donna Isabel was with them, or that, having to scramble along the rocks, they had left their weapons behind them.

"Oh, boys! if we had but a place to swim to, we'd swim rather than be caught by these baboon-faced Portugals," cried Dick, as he reluctantly re-entered the boat.

Lights were now seen as if on the water itself.

"The Portugals have launched some boats, and are coming in pursuit!" shouted Lizard.

"Never mind, lads; if we can but get through their chain, we'll hold them a long chase yet. Now, lads, a hearty pull and pull all together."

Heartily the seamen did pull, and stove in the bow of the boat, and sprang every one of their oars. With no very complimentary remarks on the Portugals' rotten spars, they broke them completely in two, and each man, grasping the inner end, prepared to use it as a quarter-staff. Scarcely had they thus armed themselves when three boats dashed up alongside them. Several voices ordered them to yield themselves prisoners.

"Yield ourselves prisoners!" exclaimed Dick. "Come and take us, you blackguards! We'll just have the pleasure of cracking some of your skulls first."

Although the Portugals did not understand Dick's polite observations, they concluded from the tone of his voice that they were not conciliatory, and therefore, with threats of vengeance, they pressed round them. Great was their astonishment and indignation as they were about to jump on board the fugitives' boat to find showers of blows descend on their heads with such hearty good-will, that with many a cracked skull they sprang back into their own boats faster than they had left them. The Portugals in the boats so thickly surrounded the English that the former could not use their fire-arms, while those on the rocks were also afraid to fire for fear of hitting their friends. Bravely and gallantly the seamen held out.

"Hurrah for the true English quarter-staves, lads!" cried Dick, as he dealt blow after blow on the heads of the Portugals, his example being ably followed by the rest of the men.

Edward shouted and encouraged his followers, though less vociferously. Several of the Portugals were knocked overboard; others, stunned, fell back into the bottom of their boats; and others, with broken arms and bruised shoulders, shouted — "Treachery! treachery! Help! help! Fire! fire!" and all sorts of cries, under the belief that the numbers of the fugitives were far greater than was the case.

As long as the enemy could be kept at close quarters the English had greatly the advantage; but at length so greatly worsted were the Portugals that the survivors and the unmaimed, getting out their oars, and shoving off from the boat which contained the audacious English, fairly took to flight, and pulled away up the harbor, maliciously shouting as they went — .

"Fire! fire at the chain!"

Their cries were heard, and the rattle of fire-arms followed, and the bright flashes were seen, while the shot whistled over the only spot at which the prisoners could hope to make their escape, even if they could manage to cut or force the chain. As it would have been certain death to make the attempt, Raymond proposed a still more daring scheme — to pull up the harbor after the Portugal boats, to board one of them before the people had recovered from their panic, to seize their arms, and then to try and make terms with the enemy, or to die fighting bravely with weapons in their hands which might be used at a longer distance than could their quarter-staves. The idea was no sooner suggested than put into execution. The boats had only gone up a short distance, and before the Portugals were aware that they were pursued, the English, with their dreaded quarter-staves, were battering away on their skulls, and in a few seconds had possessed themselves of all the fire-arms, ammunition, and swords to be found on board. Another boat was overtaken, and before those on board had recovered from their astonishment they were also deprived of their arms. The English now dashed on so as to reach the shore before their opponents, and be ready to stand on their defence. Their success was greater than they anticipated. As the Portugals were looking in other directions, no one opposed them, and they had time not only to leap on shore, but to reach a rock on the beach which Raymond recollected so close to the water that it prevented any one approaching on that side, while the rock itself formed a rampart in front, behind which they could fight. Here Edward found himself with Dick Lizard and ten other men, some of them more or less wounded, but all able to use their weapons. Although they knew that they must ultimately be starved out or overwhelmed by numbers, yet, like brave men, they agreed not to yield while resistance could by any possibility avail them. Some time passed—no enemy appeared. What were the Portugals about to do? was the question.

"They don't know where we've got to, and they're boasting that they've killed us," suggested Dick in a low voice.

Edward had still a lingering hope that they might escape. The minutes were very long, but they increased into hours, and at last the day dawned, and Dick, looking out from behind his hiding-place, could see the Portugals scattered about among the rocks near the harbor still looking for them. Daylight, however, exhibited the boat on the beach, and the marks of their feet on the sand. Their place of refuge was soon discovered, and now in numbers the Portugals came crowding up from all quarters, thinking that they were about to take their prey on easy terms, and vowing vengeance on their heads. The rock, however, formed a breastwork which no bullets could penetrate, nor even could round shot from ordnance make any impression on it. The shape was that of a half-moon, the convex side being towards the shore, with the two horns running some way into the water where it was too deep for any one to wade, except the sea was unusually smooth.

On the sea side there was deep water, outside of which was a ledge of broken rocks here and there showing their heads, forming a barrier no boats could pass, with what may be described as a lagoon of smooth water inside the rocks. Thus Raymond and his party were completely protected from the sea, unless a boat could be dragged overland and launched beyond the rock into the lagoon. This could easily have been done under ordinary circumstances, but any persons now attempting it would have been exposed to the fire of the English from the rock. Edward had noted some of the advantages offered by the rock as a place where a few determined men might defend themselves, but the strength of its position surpassed his expectations. It was the recollection of this rock which made him propose the bold attack on the Portugals in their boats which proved so successful. Some of the Portugals, it was observed, advanced bravely enough, but others, whose heads were bandaged, though they shouted and urged on their countrymen, hung back, and seemed in no way inclined to encounter the daring Englishmen. Dick Lizard pointed them out to his companions.

"Ha, ha! the varlets!" he exclaimed. "They know the flavor of our English quarter-staves, and don't want a second taste of them."

Raymond had no necessity to counsel his men to be steady, for every one had his weapons ready, and stood as cool as if no enemy were advancing to the attack. Still the number of their opponents was sufficient to daunt the stoutest hearts. Not only were there Portugals, but swarthy natives in light garments and long matchlocks, nimble fellows who looked capable of climbing over the rocks like wildcats, and proving troublesome at close quarters. There were some gayly-bedecked cavaliers on horseback, but of them the seamen took but little account.

"All we've to do, lads, is to kill the steeds, and then your horsemen become clumsy footmen," exclaimed Lizard as he saw them galloping up over the sand-hills from the interior.

The Portugals, who, like wise men, seemed to be lovers of long shots, began to fire towards the rock, not all together nor taking good aim, but as each man thought he could hit an enemy without being hit himself. The leaden bullets mostly flew high overhead, but a few came spluttering against the rock to fall flattened into the crevices or to roll down into the sand. Edward ordered his followers to keep under cover, he alone watching the progress of their foes. On they came, the showers of shots increasing in thickness, but being perfectly innocuous. The nearer they got the higher the shot flew, so that no harm was done except to the Portugals themselves by the bursting of some of their fire-arms.

"Wait, lads, till they get close up to the rock, and then fire and knock over the foremost dozen at the least," he cried out. "Maybe they won't expect the warm reception we can give them."

Raymond, like a good officer, having made the utmost of his position and taken every proper precaution to insure success, did his best to encourage his men and to make them despise their enemies. Foolish and ignorant officers neglect the necessary preparations and precautions, and yet fancy that they are exhibiting their bravery by despising their foes. This has ever been a great cause of defeat and disaster. There was a pause. The Portugals had not the heart to make a rush forward, and the English were unwilling to throw their precious shot away.

The Portugals were seen to halt, as if to hold a consultation. The perfect quietness of the English alarmed them more than loud shouting and noise would have done. They did not know what to make of it.

"Ha! ha! they've no stomach for the fight," whispered Dick, who had popped up his head to see what was going forward. "They're just thinking whether they'll go back to their wives and families, or come on and be shot. We'll teach them the wisest thing to do."

The pause was broken by the sound of a trumpet, and a cavalcade was seen approaching from the direction of the castle. As it drew near, Edward recognized by his dress and bearing Don Lobo at its head. An officer was now seen to gallop forward towards what might be called the storming party, but that they appeared to have no great inclination to storm. His message seemed to expedite their movements, and with loud shouts and a hotter fire they once more advanced. Finding also that the garrison of the rock did not reply, their courage increased as did their shouts and their speed, although it requires a stout heart to march towards an enemy over heavy sand.

"They'll go back, an' I mistake not, faster than they are coming on," whispered Dick.

"Steady, my merry men," cried Raymond as the Portugals were crowding on within a few paces of the rock.

Numbers had already begun to climb its slippery sides, pressing on each other, the hinder ones urging on those in front, the rearmost feeling their valor at the highest pitch, when Edward perceived that the time for action had arrived.

"Now, lads, give it them!" he exclaimed, setting the example by firing his piece, which was of the blunderbuss genus, rammed full of shot, and knocking over three if not more of the stormers. The rest of the party discharged their fire-arms at the same moment, lodging their contents in the bodies of some score or more of their assailants. They, the most part killed, with many who, though unhurt, were terribly alarmed, tumbled back on their comrades in the rear, all rolling down the rock together, and so thoroughly bedabbled with blood that it appeared as if the whole party were desperately wounded. This damped the courage of the rest. Some stood irresolute, others actually ran, and others shouted to their comrades to go on, but did not themselves advance. This enabled the English seamen to reload their fire-arms, and as it was evident that the fight would be carried on at close quarters, each man put as many shot into his piece as it would hold.

"Now we are ready once more for the Portugals! Hurrah, lads! give it them again!" shouted Dick, while the enemy hesitated to advance.

Several fire-arms had been taken from the boats besides those of which each man had possessed himself. These were also loaded and placed ready for use. The spirits of the seamen rose as they saw the way in which the first attack had been repulsed. Of the future they did not think. Edward, on the contrary, could not help thinking of the result, and felt that their lives must be sacrificed in the end, and that, as they had resolved to sell them dear, the longer they fought was but adding to their price. Still he kept his courage up and resolved to persevere to the end. Still the enemy did not advance. The governor was seen in the distance, and appeared to be furious at the hesitation of his men. Message after message was sent to them to goad them on. The trumpets sounded the charge, and with shouts and cries they once more advanced to climb the rock. Again Edward allowed them to approach till the most daring had got high enough to bring their breasts up to the muzzles of the pieces.

"Fire, my merry men, fire!" he shouted.

The result was even more terrible than at first, and numbers of killed and wounded men rolled back on their comrades, throwing their ranks once more into confusion. This time, however, others attempted to come on, but Edward, leaving two of his party to reload the fire-arms, led on the rest armed with their quarter-staves, and leaping on the rock gave the foe so unexpected a reception that they were driven helter-skelter back and fairly put to flight. Edward restrained his men from firing a volley after them, as ammunition was too precious to be thrown away. This success gave them a short breathing-time. Raymond had little hopes, however, of obtaining fair and honorable terms. Carrying off their wounded, but leaving their dead under the rock, the Portugals withdrew to a distance.

The Englishmen had time now to consider their position and what was to be done. They were as unanimous as at first in determining to hold out to the last gasp. Indeed, Edward reminded them that if they yielded they would certainly be put to death. Without saying any thing, Dick slipped from among the rest, and with a large knife in his hand rushed into the water. He speedily returned with a large bunch of clams and other shell-fish.

"Ha! ha! the Portugals will not starve us out as quickly as they think," he exclaimed triumphantly. "That's the reason, I take it, that they hold back."

Probably Dick was right in his conjecture. There was no want of driftwood under the rock, and, though raw shell-fish have often been eaten, even seamen prefer them cooked. A fire was soon lighted, and all the garrison were speedily employed in roasting the shell-fish. The Portugals on seeing the smoke must have guessed its cause, for they were soon again seen assembling to renew the attack. Edward saw that the time had come when they must prepare to die like brave men, for he could not hope to repulse another attack as successfully as he had done the first. Often did the brave band wish they were on the deck of a stout ship prepared to do battle on somewhat equal terms, with a prospect of victory in the end, or at worst to go down with colors flying to find their graves in the element they loved so well. Ever and anon, and naturally enough, they turned a wistful gaze over the ocean, and a sail was now descried in the horizon. The circumstance could scarcely give rise to hope, and yet often and often, as men would do, they turned their eyes in the same direction to watch her progress. She was, however, not directly approaching the shore, for the land breeze yet blew strongly off it, but she was standing along it close-hauled from the southward.

"She is edging in for the land!" cried Dick Lizard. "She may be a Portugal, or a Spaniard, or a Hollander; but oh, boys! she may — she may be an honest Englishman, and bring us help at our great need."

"The Lord grant that so it may be!" said Edward, who, without pretension, had true religious principles, and was not ashamed of his feelings. "We are in his hands. Let us pray for protection, and he will not desert us."

And then and there, on the sand and rocks, like sturdy believers as they were, they knelt down, with their arms in their hands, and humbly poured out their petition to Heaven for aid. Then they rose and looked out for the enemy. The land wind, as has been said, was blowing, and the heat was very great, especially on the sands, and the Portugals seemed rather inclined to take their siesta than to fight with enemies whom they believed they had got securely in a trap from which they could not ultimately escape death or capture.

As the sun rose the wind died away, and the heat became almost unbearable. Some of Edward's party declared that they should be roasted alive, and that they felt themselves bubbling and hissing already.

"Never mind, lads, a plunge in the sea will soon cool us; and that's what I propose we take to when our ammunition is all gone," cried Dick.

Even while he was talking, however, a ripple was

seen to play over the surface of the lagoon, and a faint breeze fanned their scorched cheeks.

"Hurrah, lads! here comes the honest sea wind," exclaimed Dick. "May it blow us good luck!"

Stronger and stronger it blew, and now the strange ship was seen to be rapidly approaching the land under all sail, having squared away her yards before it. Had the Portugals been more wide awake they would have long since seen her. They seemed, indeed, in no way disconcerted at her appearance. After a time, the Portugal flag was seen flying at her peak, and they were evidently prepared to welcome her as a friend. The hopes of most of the party again sank low. Dick, however, constantly kept his eye on the stranger, scanning her sails and rigging and lofty hull. He had not much time to engage in this agreeable occupation before Raymond called his men to their posts, for the enemy were seen mustering in great numbers, probably ashamed that their countrymen should find them kept at bay by a mere handful of foreigners. Don Lobo himself rode forth from the castle with his staff of officers, and drums beat, and trumpets brayed, and cymbals clashed as the troops rushed forward to the assault. On they came.

"Steady as before, my brave men, and we'll beat them off again," cried Edward.

Up the rock they climbed with fierce shouts and denunciations of vengeance, but the same mistake was again committed as at first — the bravest had

been allowed to go first, the more cowardly following. Again the little English band of heroes let fly their pieces, knocking over the leaders, who, falling back, threw the rest into disorder. Some struggled on, and the English quarter-staves again came into use. Several of the English were, however, wounded by the pistols of the Portugals. Raymond got a severe cut on his left arm, and a bullet went through the brain of another man. Still the seamen struggled on, and making a rush all together, drove the Portugals once more to the bottom of the rock. Now, had the cowards led the way they would have undoubtedly been killed by the volley of the English; but before the latter could reload, the braver men would have been upon them, and would probably have ended the unequal contest. As it was, so great was the awe inspired by the English seamen's determined bravery, that it was some time before the Portugals could be again brought up to the attack.

During the interval the stranger ship had approached as near the shore as it was safe to venture, and had there cast anchor, just beyond the range of the guns of the castle. Several boats were seen to be lowered from her lofty sides. They were at once filled with men and pulled towards the shore, under cover of the ship's guns. The ship had come to an anchor while the fighting was going forward, and no sooner were the enemy repulsed than Lizard turned his eyes towards the ocean to ascertain what the stranger was about. He took a steady gaze at her, and then giving a loud slap with his hand on his thigh, he exclaimed —

"The Lion, lads, the Lion! Hurrah! Old England for ever! Hurrah!"

His shouts made all his companions turn their eyes in the same direction, and so asborbed were they in gazing at the stranger, that had the enemy stormed at that moment the little English band would have been cut to pieces. A second glance was not necessary to convince Edward that the ship he saw was indeed the Lion herself.

The Portugals, it seemed by their movements, began to have some suspicions of the character of the stranger, and of the object of the boats in coming on shore. It made them still more eager to recapture their former prisoners, and to retire to the fort. Doubly resolved, however, were Raymond and his men to hold out till their countrymen could come to their rescue. The boats were steering for a bay between the rock and the castle. Again the Portugals began to assail the rock with fierce cries of vengeance. The seamen shouted in return. Hotter and hotter grew the fight; the eleven defenders of the rock stood boldly at bay, hurling the Portugals down the rock, casting their pistols, which they snatched from their hands, after them, and often bringing their own quarter-staves into play. Still, from loss of blood and the constant attacks of the enemy, their strength began to fail; even Edward felt that nature would give way, when the stranger's boats reached the beach. Each boat was full of men, who leaped on shore and formed in two parties — one pushing towards the castle, the other, shouting "St. George and Merry England!" towards the rock. On they came. There was no doubt that they were friends. Some of the Portugals faced about to meet them; but so furiously did the strangers charge, that, after exchanging several blows, resulting in not a few cracked skulls, those who could run took to their heels and fled. Edward, seeing this, charged down on his assailants, driving them before him to the bottom of the rock, which his friends at the same moment reached. The remainder of the enemy, finding themselves between two fires, made no attempt at defence, but as many as could escape ran off inland, the rest being cut to pieces or made prisoners.

Hearty were the greetings as shipmates, long separated, clasped the hands of shipmates — for the new-comers were the brave Lions. Raymond's first inquiry was for Antony Waymouth.

"The captain is leading the other party," was the answer. "Our orders are to push on to join him."

"Oh, let us go!" cried Edward, forgetting his wounds, fatigue, and every thing, and eager only to join his friend.

On they went over the hot sands, not altogether

unmolested; for the Portugals fired at them from a distance, and here and there one of the party was hit; but no one seemed to care for wounds — the Castle of San Pedro, with the reputed riches of its savage governor, was to be their prize. The two parties met under the walls. There was a short but hearty greeting between Antony Waymouth and Edward Raymond.

"We have no lack of gold and jewels already aboard the Lion," exclaimed the former; "but an' we become masters of what this castle holds we may turn our bows homeward, and no longer go roaming the world around for gold; that those who have lady-loves may wed and live like lords of the land to the end of their days. Yet I tell thee, Ned, I am more glad to see thee alive and hearty than if I had gained this fortress."

There was no time for Edward to tell his story. Waymouth assured him that, had he suspected he was with the defenders of the rock, he should have come in person to his assistance. Waymouth's party had landed with some scaling-ladders and a small ram used for battering open gates. The men were all eager to begin the attack. They had halted under shelter of some rocks near the forts. With a loud cheer the men sprang forward as the bugles sounded for the assault. Some placed the scaling-ladders against the walls, and began to climb up with a celerity and activity which only seamen can display; others bore on the battering-ram towards one of the gates, which they battered with vigorous blows; while a third party, armed with arquebuses and cross-bows, shot bullets and bolts towards the walls, bringing down all who appeared upon them.

Although, from so great a number of the Portugals having been put to flight, the defenders were few, the walls were high and the gates strong, and, to get into the castle was no easy matter. As to the gate, the Portugals let the battering-ram do its worst without interfering, while they united all their efforts in opposing the escaladers, who, as they reached the summit of the ladders, again and again were hurled down, some with broken heads and gashed shoulders and arms, and others killed outright, though not a few were ready, as at first, to climb up and renew the attack.

Waymouth and his officers exerted themselves gallantly, but discovered that stone walls are hard things for men to knock their heads against, and many began to fear that the exploit must be abandoned, when Edward, who, in spite of his wound, had not been behindhand in exhibiting his courage, recollected the gate out of which Donna Isabel had conducted him the previous night, and the angle of the wall down which he had slipped. Telling Waymouth what he proposed doing, he summoned Dick Lizard and some of his companions in captivity, with a few other fresh men, and, briefly explaining his plans, led them round close under the walls on the sand where it was evidently generally washed by the sea. The angle was reached, and by the rope which Edward had left hanging over when making his escape he prepared to climb up, though each of his men was eager to lead. Young Marston, who was the only midshipman of the party, especially entreated that he might go.

"I'll be at the top in a moment, sir," he whispered. "I'll let you know if there are any Portugals near, and if they tumble me over it will matter nothing."

Edward, however, would allow no one to precede him. He grasped the rope, and began his ascent. How different were his feelings from what they had been when descending a few hours before! Marston followed directly after him. Up he climbed, expecting every moment a Portugal's head to appear over the parapet, and to see the rope cut above him. On he went, though. The summit was reached, and throwing himself on it, he drew his sword and stood ready to defend the spot till his men should have likewise gained a footing. Marston was by his side in a moment. When they looked around, not a Portugal was to be seen to stop their progress. Forward they rushed accordingly, and got half way across the open before they were discovered by one of the garrison. The man who first saw them summoned others, and a pretty strong party was collected to oppose them, who, rushing down, met them before they reached the gate at which they were aiming. So furiously, however, did the seamen charge the enemy, that they were driven back, cut down, or put to flight before any one had time to shut the gate, which, as Edward had hoped might be the case, was left open. A few rushed in before them, and a desperate struggle ensued. In the end not a Portugal remained alive. The passages resounded with the tramp of armed men, the clash of steel, the reports of pistols, and the cries of the wounded, while clouds of smoke rolled along them.

"On! on!" was the cry.

Dick Lizard happily knew the way to the principal gate.

"I'll tell you, Master Raymond, by and by how I came to know it," he remarked. "It's all of the lady who helped us out."

On they went. It was every thing to reach the principal gate without further opposition. As Edward had hoped, all the defenders were on the ramparts. No one had remained inside the gate, which from its strength it was supposed would withstand any attempt to batter it down. Dick was not mistaken. The thundering of the battering-ram guided them also to the spot. Passing under a broad archway, they found themselves just within the great gate. The din of the battle outside had prevented their approach being heard, while every one was too busy to observe them. Bars and bolts innumerable guarded the gate. These Edward and his followers began to withdraw, but they were so huge and rusty that it was with difficulty they could be removed. While the seamen were still laboring away, Raymond, turning his head, saw at the farther end of the passage a number of men approaching. At their head he recognized Don Lobo himself. With cries of vengeance, the governor led on his men. The blood of the Lusitanian was up, and, cruel tyrant and extortioner as he had been, when he found himself pushed to extremities, and his enemies already within his stronghold, he resolved to drive them out or die as became him in its defence. As the governor approached, Edward and part of his company faced about to encounter him, while Dick Lizard and the rest plied crowbars and hammers in beating back the huge bolts which secured the gate. The battering-ram was all the time thundering away outside. The object of Don Lobo was to destroy the daring band of Englishmen who had got inside, and to replace the bolts before the ram had forced the gate. Nobly Edward and his little party kept their numerous foes, hard pressing on them, at bay. Don Lobo himself rushed forward at length in desperation, and his blade crossed that of Edward.

"Ha, ha! I hate you, and you know the reason, vile Englishman!" he exclaimed, as he made a lunge at his opponent's breast.

Edward turned the weapon aside, and that instant Dick shouted —

"Stand from under, lads! stand from under!"

For the huge gate was cracking in every part,

and with a loud crash down it came, crushing one poor fellow, the rest with difficulty escaping. Don Lobo heard the shout and the crash. His eye was for an instant withdrawn from his sword's point to look at the falling gate. That instant was fatal to him, and Edward's weapon entering his bosom, he fell backwards to the ground, while his own sword fell useless from his grasp. As the gate gave way, the fierce and eager countenances of the English seamen were seen in the entrance, led on by Waymouth.

"St. George and merry England!" they shouted. "Down with the Portugals! Hurrah! hurrah!"

"An' you cry 'Down with the Portugals!' just be sure if there are Portugals to put down," cried Dick. "The mouse has got into the cheese before you, mates; but there is no lack of mites yet to eat. On — on, lads!"

Dick narrowly escaped a clout on the head by his facetiousness. Fortunately, daylight came in through the open gateway, and through the smoke and dust his features were recognized in time. The whole party now rushed forward. Some of the Portugals in narrow passages made a stand, but they were forced back and driven from chamber to chamber till every part of the castle was in the hands of the English.

"The miser's gold! the miser's gold!" was now the cry. "Where are his strong boxes? Bring him forth, and make him tell us."

Several hurried off to search for the late governor. Edward might have told them of his fate, but he, mindful of poor Don Joao, had gone to look for his unfortunate acquaintance, and to save him, if possible, from insult or violence.

Here and there the sound of strife might still be heard as a few of the braver spirits who had retreated, not aware how entirely the castle was in the power of the English, were defending themselves in rooms and galleries from small parties of adventurers who had separated from the main body in search of plunder.

Edward had made inquiries both of Portugals and English if they knew aught of Don Joao. At length, led by the sound of clashing steel, he found his way, with the few men he had got to follow him, into the circular chamber of a distant tower. There in a deep window recess clustered three or four priests holding crucifixes in their hands, some dark-skinned women in their picturesque costume, and some native attendants. Before them stood Don Joao, with five or six Portugal soldiers, defending themselves with their swords against the attacks of four or five English sailors, who were hewing and hacking away, not with much science, but with such furious blows that they had already cut down two or more Portugals, and were now hard pressing the old soldier. He was bleeding from more than one wound, and was evidently little able to hold out against assailants so persevering. Edward hurried forward, ordering the Englishmen to desist; but they either would not or did not hear him, and before he could interpose his own weapon, a heavy cut from a rapier brought the old man to the ground.

"For shame, men!" exclaimed Edward, saving the old soldier from another blow. "We war not with gray hairs, with priests and women. Let not another blow be struck."

The Portugals, finding resistance hopeless, threw down their arms. Edward knelt down by the old man's side, and raised his head. It was very evident that his last hours were passing by.

"My daughter?" he asked in a faint voice. "Brave Englishman, can you tell me any thing of my daughter? She had my leave to aid in your escape. I would have accompanied her had I been able."

Edward felt sick at heart at having to tell the poor father of his daughter's fate. Yet what could he say?

"Alas! I cannot say but I fear the worst," was his reply.

"I dreaded to hear this, but do not blame you, noble Englishman. The last link which bound me to earth is broken, and I am ready to quit this world, which man's folly and wickedness has made so full of woe and suffering."

These were almost the last words the old man spoke, though the priests came round and administered the rites of their faith ere his spirit quitted its frail tenement. Even the rough seamen, despisers and haters of all papistical ceremonies, looked on with respect and awe as the old soldier's head sank on his breast, and his hand fell powerless by his side.

Waymouth had taken precautions to secure all the entrances to the castle while the garrison were committed to the dungeons in which they had been accustomed to confine the enemies who had the misfortune of falling into their hands. Those who had gone in search of Don Lobo soon returned, bearing on a litter his dead body, an officer holding up in triumph a bunch of keys which had been found in his pockets, and shouting —

"The keys of his money-chests! the keys of his money-chests!"

"The keys are but of small service to us without the chests," remarked the captain. "Find the chests, men, and we may make small account of the keys."

A diligent search was therefore commenced for the reputed wealth of the old governor. It was said that he had employed thirty years in collecting it, and that he had purposed shortly returning to Europe, under the vain belief that it would afford him enjoyment and contentment. Every passage, and corner, and crevice of the castle from top to bottom was searched, and not a sign of a money-box could be discovered. Some declared that the governor's wealth was really fabulous — that is to say, it had no existence; while others affirmed that it did exist, and would somewhere be discovered. Midshipmen generally consider hunting for rabbits very good fun, but hunting for money-chests was very much better. All the cabin-boys of the Lion hunted round and round and up and down with wonderful zeal. The captain at last promised that whoever found the wealth should have a tenth portion of it. This still further excited the diligence of all hands. Still no chests were forthcoming. Some, in revenge, proposed burning down the castle, till the captain announced that whoever set it on fire should be cast into the flames. Again and again the search was renewed. The prisoners were interrogated, but no one could tell. Rewards were offered without effect. It was evident that they did not know. Several said that Pedro Pacheco knew; but that worthy had been run through the body by a pike, which had struck him in the back as he was making his escape with a bag of gold under his arm, which he refused to stop and deliver. The booty was, after all, not so contemptible, for there were silver plate in large quantities, and jewelled ornaments, and golden coin; but, as it was not what was expected, no one was contented.

At last Oliver Marston happened to strike his foot against a ring in the corner of a small room on the ground floor of the castle. It served as the handle of a stone which without difficulty he lifted. Lights were brought. A flight of stone steps led to a vault, in which was an iron door. Crowbars, eagerly brought, forced it open, and there exposed to view were a dozen large iron chests. The governor's keys were applied, the lids opened, and exposed to view ingots of gold and silver, and jewels and coins scarcely to be counted. Wild were the shouts of delight as chest after chest was opened, and each one in succession appeared to contain more gold and jewels than the first. The chests were computed to contain property of even greater value than what was already on board the Lion. It was no easy work to carry off the chests, but it was accomplished before the eyelids of one of the victors closed in sleep. The prisoners were allowed their liberty, the castle was set on fire, and, while the flames were bursting out on all sides, the Lion made sail with her rich freight, and stood away to the southward.

CHAPTER VIII.

Away sailed the Lion, those on board exulting in the rich booty they had obtained, and looking ere many months had passed by once more to tread the shores of Old England and to enjoy the wealth they had gotten with so much toil and danger. Good Master Walker, the minister, did his best to warn them not to trust to the riches they had acquired, that riches are apt to take to themselves wings and flee away, and that it in no way follows that because people possess wealth they will have the power of enjoying it. These and other similar remarks were received by the officers and men in general with no good grace, and Master Walker lost popularity simply because no one could deny the truth of his remarks.

"There is many a slip between the cup and the lip," he added one day, most greatly to the annoyance of his hearers.

The more conscious people are that a thing may probably come to pass, the more angry they are, if it is against their wish that it should happen, when they are told so. Antony Waymouth was no despiser of gold — or rather the good things of life which gold procures — but he loved his honor more, and he considered it his duty to go in search of the commander-in-chief and the rest of the fleet, if haply they might have reached the rendezvous at Bantam. Waymouth had full experience of the responsibility of power, though he had able assistants in Raymond and his first officer, Carlingford. Several of the crew had for many months shown a mutinous disposition, though the storms to which they had been exposed, the fights in which they had been engaged, and the prospect of the attack on the Castle of San Pedro, had prevented any serious outbreak. Now, however, they loudly expressed their disapproval of continuing the search for Captain Wood, declaring that he and his consorts must long since have perished, and that they, having collected so large an amount of wealth, would be acting like fools to remain out a day longer than they could help. Round the mess-table by day and during the watches of the night the only subject of conversation was the way in which they would spend their wealth when they got on shore. Their disappointment and anger therefore increased greatly when they found that the time for their return might be indefinitely delayed. Those even who had hitherto been obedient began to express themselves in a mutinous manner, and to hint that the sooner another man was captain the better it would be for all hands fore and aft. This state of things was not unknown to Waymouth and his officers, and it put them on their guard; but while no overt act was committed, it was impossible to take active steps to bring about a change. As at first, Peter Hagger, the boatswain, with his mate and Dick Soper, a seaman, were supposed to be the ringleaders. Though narrowly watched, nothing could be proved against them. The captain's two cabin-boys, Oliver Marston and Alfred Stanhope, proud of the approval they had before received, determined to discover, if possible, what was wrong. They had taken Dick Lizard into their councils, assured that he, at all events, might be depended on. In spite of all their wealth and their anticipations of the pleasures it might procure, none of either high or low degree on board could boast of much enjoyment. The happiest person was Master Walker. He was doing his duty, and leaving the consequences in the hand of Heaven. The Island of Java was once more sighted and the Harbor of Bantam entered. No certain news could there be obtained of Captain Wood. Several large ships of the Hollanders had, however, visited the place since their departure, and the people had done their best to spread evil reports of the English. Waymouth cared little for this, but he vowed, should he ever come across the Hollanders, he would make them pay for their slanders, and those who knew him best had no doubt that he would put his threat into execution. Still his chief desire was to go in search of his friends, but even this could not be done without delay, for, he having ordered a survey of the Lion, the carpenters reported that she must undergo a thorough repair before she would be fit to put to sea. No man knew better than the bold captain of the Lion how to get into the good graces of people in power, and he soon gained the confidence and good-will of the King of Bantam. At the same time he was too wise to put more confidence in his majesty than was necessary; he therefore carefully kept concealed from him the amount of wealth the Lion had on board, and rather let him suppose that he and his company were needy adventurers who had yet their fortunes to make at the point of their swords, at the same time that the little they possessed they were ready to expend liberally. This policy answered so well that the repairs of the Lion were allowed to proceed without interruption.

One enemy, however, could by no means be kept at a distance. It was the black fever. While still many necessary repairs were yet to be done, it made its baneful appearance. Strong men who had boldly confronted the fiercest foes and the raging storm turned pale when they heard that it had already carried off six of their shipmates. From that time not a day passed but two or more died. Every one of the company labored hard to get the ship ready for sea, under the belief that they should leave the fell destroyer behind them. Now the qualities of Master Walker, the chaplain, shone forth brightly, for while others shrank back from attending on the plague-stricken, he boldly went among the sick and attended the dying, giving them spiritual counsel and consolation, tending them, and administering medicines prescribed by the surgeon. Full thirty of her brave crew had succumbed to the destroyer, before the Lion, having been got ready for sea, once more ploughed the waters of the ocean. Still the fever raged. Gladly would those on board have given all their wealth to have escaped with health from the plague-stricken ship. Day after day more and more were called away. A small number only of those who were attacked survived, but so sick and weak did they remain that their recovery was hardly expected.

Waymouth had received intimation that some ships, supposed to be English, had been seen farther to the eastward, and from the description given, believing them to be Captain Wood's squadron, he steered a course in that direction. On sailed the Lion on her solitary course. The Angel of Death still pursued her, continuing to summon one after another of her crew. Hope of finding his consorts, however, allured the brave captain on in spite of the ravages of the plague and the warnings given him of the increasing discontent of the crew.

"I know the varlets, and fear them not," he answered. "I showed them before who was master, and will show them again to their cost."

Meantime, Peter Hagger, the boatswain, had been biding his time and strengthening his party by every device he could think of. He well knew that he was watched, but he strove to throw the captain off his guard by a frankness of manner, an unusual attention to his duties, and the strictness with which all orders were obeyed. He appeared to have succeeded so far as to make Waymouth believe that he had abandoned his evil designs, and might be trusted. In the fore part of the ship, far down in her inward depths, was situated his principal storeroom. There the light of day had never entered since the huge structure had been put together, nor had fresh air penetrated. It was redolent of pitchy and tarry odors, with numerous others of a far from fragrant character. A large horn lantern hung from a beam above, and shed a sickly light throughout the chamber. Here, seated on chests and casks, with their heads bent forward together as if in earnest consultation, were about a dozen seamen. Their naturally ill-favored countenances were not improved by long exposure to the burning sun of the tropics. The presiding spirit among them was evidently Peter Hagger, the boatswain.

"Are we all agreed, mates?" he asked in his usual gruff voice.

"All," said several. "Provided we take no lives," added others. "The fever has been doing enough of that work lately among us."

"Dead men tell no tales," observed Hagger.

"If we secure the gold we need fear neither dead

nor living men," observed one of the men, who, from the tone of his voice, was evidently of superior education to the rest. "If they were ever to come back without a stiver in their pockets, who would take their word against ours, when we are rolling in wealth?"

"But if we don't heave them overboard or run them up to the yard-arm, what are we to do with them?" was a question put by another speaker.

"Why, land them on a desolate island, or sell them to some of these Easterns, or put them on board a prize with provisions to take them to the nearest shore, that would be giving them a fair chance of escape, and no one need complain," was the remark of a mutineer who had sided with Hagger.

"That will do," observed the boatswain. "And now, mates, the sooner we set about this work the better. To my mind there's no time like the present. Every day we are going farther and farther to the eastward, and every day getting more and more out of our reckoning. Now d'ye see? All we've to do is to sail west, and when we get into the longitude of Bon Esperanza Cape, steer north, and we'll find our way back to Old England, never fear."

"Ay, ay! with you as captain, Master Hagger," exclaimed several mutineers, "we shall go straight forward, not be running here and there, looking into this port and that port, and all to no purpose, to look for people who have long since gone to Davy

Jones's locker. Peter Hagger for captain! He's the man we want."

Peter Hagger bent forward, for the height of the cabin did not allow him to stand upright.

"Mates, I take your terms," he said in a low voice. "I've no wish to injure any man, least of all Master Waymouth, who has good qualities, I'll allow; but we must have our rights, and if he has lost his wits — as there's no doubt he has — it is seemly that some better man should take his place, and as you choose me, mates, why, I'm not the man to gainsay you."

"All right, Captain Hagger; all right," said several of the men. "But what is it you would have us do?"

"That's what I was coming to," answered Hagger, still more lowering his voice till it was only audible to those who put their ears close to his mouth.

The men talked long and earnestly together, till all their plans seemed matured. Not only were their plans matured, but they appeared confident of success. One by one they stole off from their place of meeting. They had no fear of having been overheard, for, suspecting that such had before been the case, they had now placed sentries to give notice of the approach of any one they might suspect. Separating, they went to their hammocks, and, what may seem strange, all except the arch-mutineer slept as soundly as if their consciences were free from blame. He could not rest; for though he believed that he was on the point of obtaining the object of his desires — the larger portion of the store of wealth contained in the Lion — yet all the time he was conscious that he had not the ability to retain command over the lawless band who had selected him as their leader, nor the knowledge necessary to navigate the ship to an English port. Still he was determined to persevere in his mad course. He trusted to chance for the future. The wealth he was resolved to have at all risks. The following night had been fixed on for the outbreak.

It was the middle watch. The weather even for those latitudes was hot and close. Many of the officers found their cabins too warm to allow them to sleep, and had come on deck to endeavor to obtain rest. Some had thrown themselves down in spots where they were unobserved, and had gone to sleep. Miles Carlingford had charge of the watch, with the two young cabin-boys, Stanhope and Marston, under him. The captain, accompanied by Edward Raymond, after a time came also on deck. Waymouth cast his eyes round the horizon several times as he slowly paced up and down with Raymond.

"I like not the look of the midnight sky," he observed to Carlingford; "I have known black storms, with fury so terrible that scarcely the stoutest ships could withstand them, spring out of such. We must be on the watch. With our weakened crew we cannot shorten sail as we were wont to do, and yet I would not rouse up the men unnecessarily."

"Ay, ay, sir, I'll not let my eyes wink," answered Carlingford; "but I hope the weather may clear without the storm. Still, there is no telling in these latitudes what may happen. I would we were out of them."

"So do I, Master Carlingford, believe me, most heartily," answered the captain. "I promise you, too, that if in two days we do not discover the admiral we will shape a course for the Cape of Bon Esperanza; after recruiting ourselves there we will lose no time in sailing for Old England."

"It will be a happy time indeed, sir, when we again see the white cliffs of our native land," remarked Raymond, anxious to keep his chief up to his intentions. "I would that the crew were made acquainted with your intentions; it would tranquillize their minds, and banish the discontent in which they now indulge."

"They will know in good time," answered Waymouth, somewhat angrily. "It does not do to yield to their fancies, or they will become masters over those they are bound to obey."

Scarcely had he spoken when from each of the hatchways, which had been left open on account of the heat, numerous dark forms sprang up, though so silently that neither did he nor the other officers who were looking seaward hear or observe them. Like tigers on their prey the men threw themselves on the knot of officers, who were instantly brought violently to the deck, and pinioned before they had time to cry out. In vain they struggled; they were dragged to the guns, to one of which Waymouth, Carlingford, Raymond, and the two cabin-boys were securely lashed almost before the rest of the officers on deck had sprung to their feet, aroused by the cries they made. None had arms; and the rest of the mutineers, rushing aft, grappled with them, threatening vengeance if they resisted. Surprised and bewildered by the suddenness of the attack, scarcely aware by whom it was made, they were easily knocked down and secured.

The Welsh surgeon, Ap Reece, was below, sleeping soundly in spite of the heat and the noise, fatigued with his attendance on the sick, who were still numerous. The shouts and cries of his struggling brother officers awoke him, and, seizing a rapier and a brace of pistols, which he stuck in his belt, he was about to spring on deck to their assistance, when it occurred to him that it would be wiser to ascertain exactly what was occurring. The words which reached his ears — " Mutiny! mutiny! Help! help! Loyal men to the rescue!" — showed him clearly the state of the case.

" The scoundrels will be waiting to knock all who are below on the head as they come up," he thought to himself; " but I will disappoint them."

Thereon he began to make his way forward, where he was sure of finding some of the men ready to side with him. There was a passage from one end of the ship to the other, and at the division between the officers' quarters and the fore-part a sentry was usually placed, but sickness had so diminished the numbers of the crew that there were not enough men to perform any but the most necessary duties. Ap Reece groped his way on in darkness. He heard some men haHooing out, but it was evident that they were bound, and could render him no assistance till they were released. On a sudden a hand grasped his arm.

"Who is this?" said a voice which he recognized as that of honest Dick Lizard.

"A friend to all hands," answered the surgeon. "I hope that you have not turned mutineer, Dick."

"No, indeed, I should hope not, sir," replied Dick indignantly; "I have a guess of what's going on. What can we do to help the officers? All the true men are bound hand and foot, and I'm the only one who managed to slip away."

"We won't despair, Dick; are you armed?" asked the surgeon.

"I've a hanger, sir," was the answer.

"Come here and I'll give you some pistols," said Ap Reece. "Now we'll first loose all the true men, and then make a rush together and release the captain, if we can find him. With a sword in his hand he'll soon give good account of the mutineers and bring them to terms."

The surgeon, stepping back, armed Dick as he

had promised, and together they found their way without interruption to the fore-hatch. As they got their heads up to the coamings they perceived that the scuffling had ceased, though the voices of a few of the officers were heard upbraiding the men for their treachery.

"My friends, I beseech you to be silent. Let me speak to these misguided men," said a voice which they recognized to be that of Master Walker, the minister. "Mutineers! — for such you are — you are triumphing now in the success of your scheme, and the fancied possession of all the wealth this ship contains; but first let me ask you what does it advantage you now? Nothing. What can it ever advantage you? You can never enjoy it; for be assured that the vengeance of Heaven will overtake you sooner or later; even now, wretched men, it is preparing for you."

"Cease, cease, Master Walker," exclaimed Hagger, stepping up to the minister. "We wish you no ill; necessity makes us act as we do. We want to injure no one, but we won't stand opposition, and I for one cannot be answerable for the consequences."

It is needless to say that this threat was accompanied by numerous oaths which need not be repeated; in truth, Peter Hagger never spoke without interlarding his remarks with expressions of that description.

Ap Reece guessed correctly that the appeal of

Master Walker would have no present beneficial effect, and therefore he and Lizard slipped down below again and made their way to the cabins of some of the inferior officers whom the latter believed had not joined in the mutiny. Two of them, the gunner and carpenter, were found lashed in their berths, not having the slightest conception of what had occurred, and believing that they were the only sufferers. A few brief words explained matters to them. Three other men who had positively refused to join the mutiny were found lashed in different parts of the ship. They were releasd, hangers were placed in their hands, and, together, led by Ap Reece, they sprang on deck and rushed aft to where the officers lay bound, their principal object being to release Captain Waymouth and then to attack the mutineers.

As they were on their way, a shout and a loud oath from Hagger, who saw them coming, called the attention of his followers, the boatswain throwing himself before the captain at the moment Ap Reece was about with his hanger to sever the lashings which bound him. The surgeon was therefore compelled to use his weapon to defend his own life, for the boatswain, seeing what he was about, attacked him with the greatest fury, and a desperate combat ensued. Lizard and the other men, foiled in their attempt to release some of the officers, were fighting for their lives. Dick and his party were, however, able to keep their immediate opponents at bay, the chief interest centring between Ap Reece and the boatswain. Hagger was a huge, powerful man, with a round bullet-head covered by black shaggy hair, and a face of the bull-dog type. Ap Reece, on the contrary, was a slight active man, but he made up by activity what he wanted in strength. He, too, had science, which the boatswain had not, and altogether the combatants were not unevenly matched. The great strength of the boatswain gave him, however, somewhat the advantage, as he wisely only stood on the defensive, allowing the surgeon to exhaust his powers. Ap Reece sprang round and round him — now he retreated, now he advanced, but to no purpose — Hagger was not to be betrayed into abandoning his tactics. He waited his opportunity. It came. The surgeon's foot slipped, and unable to recover himself, his knees came with great force on the deck. At that instant a flash of lightning darting from the clouds revealed the combatants to each other.

"Hagger, I saved your life once when all hope seemed gone," exclaimed Ap Reece, as the mutineer's weapon was about to descend on his head. "I don't ask for my life from you or such a one as you. Strike, and add a gross act of folly to your crimes and madness. But the fever has not left the ship yet; and the time will come ere long when you and your comrades in your night's work will want my aid, and will be ready to give for it all the gold you have got in your possession. Strike, I say."

The boatswain's hanger was again lifted as if to strike, when one of his own party sprang forward.

"Hold, hold, Master Hagger," he cried out, interposing his own weapon. "Our surgeon speaks the truth. We, any one of us, may want doctoring ere an hour be over, and who's to doctor us an' we trust to Tim Rosemerry, who swears he knows the whole art, from having served an apprenticeship for six months to a foreign leech in the city of Westminster? I put it, mates, are we to have a doctor who knows nothing, or a friend who has set many of us on his legs when we thought that we were never to walk again?"

"Let the doctor live! let the doctor live!" exclaimed all the men, surrounding the boatswain, who dropped the point of his weapon.

"Thanks, friends. I accept my life, for I have no wish to lose it," said Ap Reece, rising to his feet. "The sick I will doctor as before; but remember, I will sanction no act of violence or cruelty while I remain with you."

"Oh, we are all honorable men here," cried several of the men in a derisive tone, to which remark the surgeon thought it imprudent to reply.

While this scene was acting, Dick Lizard and his companions were exchanging blows with the rest of the mutineers; but overwhelmed by numbers, two were killed, and Dick and another were brought to the deck badly wounded. Dick had been a general favorite; and although the mutineers were exasperated with him for the attack he had made on them, and for the unmeasured abuse he now heaped on their heads, they agreed he was too good a fellow to be put out of the way, and that if he would keep a civil tongue in his head, he should live. This was a somewhat difficult task for honest Dick, though, when his life was offered, like a wise man he accepted it without thinking it necessary to make any stipulations.

The mutineers had now decidedly gained the day; the officers were forced at the sword's point to go below, and each was confined in his own cabin. The threatening state of the weather made Hagger anxious to arrange matters. There was no wind, but an ominous swell had got up which made the ship roll heavily, and loud claps of thunder rattled through the sky, while vivid flashes of forked lightning darted from the clouds, hissing like fiery serpents along the surface of the ocean, or playing round the masts and threatening the Lion with destruction.

Waymouth lay in his cabin, feeling like a chained beast of the forest eager to be loose, indignant at the treachery practised on him, and feeling also the probability that the ignorant men who had been guilty of this act of atrocity would wreck the ship, and involve both themselves and him and his officers in a common destruction. He knew that they were totally unaware of the intricacies of the navigation through which the Lion had got so far to the eastward, and that it would be impossible for them unaided to retrace their course. He had perhaps a grim satisfaction in contemplating this, though all his own prospects of wealth would vanish, and life itself be lost. At length, however, the very intensity of his feelings overcame him, and he fell asleep. His sleep was far from refreshing, and his dreams were strangely troubled. Yet on he slept for some time, he believed. Whenever he felt himself waking, he forced himself to doze off again rather than awake to the disagreeable realities of his position. At length, however, the violent rolling and pitching of the ship roused him completely up. The roar of the sea, the howling of the wind, the dashing of the waves on the side of the ship, the rattling of blocks and ropes, and the tramp and shouts of men overhead, convinced him that the long-expected strife of the elements had begun. The rolling and pitching and jerking of the ship became more and more violent, the washing of the water up the sides and over the deck showed him that the sea was running high, and the way in which the ship occasionally heeled over showed him that the gale was blowing furiously. The sounds which reached him from the deck told him also that efforts were being made to shorten sail.

"The mutinous varlets! Now is the occasion to

prove their seamanship, if they have any," he muttered to himself. "What the idiots will do it is hard to say, except let the good ship drive on the rocks. What are they about now? There's not one of them can stow the mainsail properly but Hagger in a gale like this. They'll capsize the stout ship, or send the masts over the sides—the idiots!"

Thus he spoke, or rather thought, for some time. The ship plunged on through the mountainous seas, her timbers creaking and groaning as if they were about to be torn asunder. The cabin was in obscurity, for all the hatches were battened down, and not without good reason, for the foaming seas often broke so completely over the ship that without this precaution she might have filled and gone bodily down. Waymouth believed that the day was advancing from the sensations of hunger which he was beginning to experience. In vain he tried to release himself from the ropes which bound him. The more he struggled the tighter they became. Nor could he manage to get his mouth down to any part of the rope, or he would have tried to gnaw it asunder with his teeth. He shouted over and over again to his friends in captivity; but though the sound of his voice reached them, he could not, from the noises in the interior of the ship, make out what they said in return. They were evidently as securely bound as he was, and also confined in their cabins.

"Patience is a virtue, I doubt not, but it is sore

difficult to exercise it just now," he said to himself, with a mocking laugh.

Suddenly the ship heeled over more than ever — there was a loud crash — the sea seemed with fierce roars to be washing over her — shrieks and cries of distress reached his ears even where he lay. Again she righted, and seemed to go tearing on through the ocean as before.

"One or more of our masts have gone," muttered Waymouth. "Well, let them go; it is but the beginning of the end. The sooner those scoundrels find out their folly the better. Had we shortened sail as I was about to do, this disaster would have been avoided."

On, on went the ship, plunging down, again to be lifted up, truly reeling to and fro like a drunken man. Once more she was pressed down; another fearful crash followed, and there were piercing shrieks and cries. Waymouth believed fully that the ship was foundering; but no, she rose again, and rushed on still more unsteadily than before. On, on she went. Time was pressing. A hatch was removed for an instant, and a gleam of light penetrated into the cabin. Again it was obscured, and a lantern was lighted; three or four men descended. Waymouth heard them go to his lieutenant's cabin. They were offering him the command, if he would help them out of their difficulties. An indignant refusal was the reply.

"Scoundrels that you are, you may all sink with

us before I'll take charge of the ship while the rightful commander remains alive," said Carlingford.

They then applied to Raymond, who was known to be a good navigator. His reply was of the same nature. None of the temptations the mutineers could hold out would induce an officer of any rank acquainted with navigation to take command. A consultation was then held, and after some time the mutineers approached the cabin where Waymouth lay. The light of a lantern flashed on his eyes, and, the door opening, Hagger, Soper, and other mutineers stood before him.

"What is your pleasure with me, knaves?" he asked in a haughty, undaunted tone.

"An' please your honor, the ship is driving we know not where, and is like to strike on some strange rock or island, if she go not down first," said Hagger, holding his hat in his hand.

"Maybe: it is what I expected," answered Waymouth calmly. "When fools take the helm, they are certain to steer to destruction."

"An' please your honor, we wish to know whether you will please to take charge of the ship, and save her and all on board," said Soper humbly.

"Likely enough — to have my throat cut, and the throats of the gentlemen with me, by you mutinous varlets, when you find the ship in safety," answered Waymouth. "No, knaves; you have brought yourselves into this strait, and you may get out of it as best you may."

"If your honor will take command and save the ship, and overlook our conduct, we will be obedient in future," said Soper, who acted as spokesman.

"Seize that man, then, and put him in irons first," answered Waymouth, casting his glance on Hagger, who clapped his hand on his hanger, as if about to defend himself, but the rest threw themselves on him, and bore him in spite of his great strength to the deck.

"Now haste and release my officers, and beg them to come here," continued Waymouth, addressing one of the men who was not required to hold the chief mutineer.

Raymond, Carlingford, Master Walker, Ap Reece, and the other officers quickly made their appearance, surprised at the turn matters had taken. In their presence he made the mutineers cast off his fetters, and ordering Hagger to be bound and secured in a place of safety, he exclaimed, "Follow me, gentlemen!" and sprang with an elastic step on deck. The scene which met his eye was, however, far from encouraging. Two of the masts had gone by the board, and now hung with a mass of rigging and shattered spars over the sides. Part of the foremast only was standing, on which the foresail was set, driving the ship on furiously through the water, while the seas, foaming up on either hand, threatened to overwhelm her, and sent the masts and spars dashing like battering-rams against the sides as if about to stave them in. All the boats were gone or knocked to pieces, and booms and caboose — indeed, the sea had made a clean sweep of every thing movable on deck. Fearfully, too, was the number of the crew diminished — not a dozen mutineers remained alive; the rest had been carried away when the masts fell, or had been swept off the decks by the raging seas which had broken on board. The officers and men who had remained faithful outnumbered the mutineers. It appeared, however, that human skill and courage would be but of little avail, and that the gallant ship was doomed to destruction.

"The scoundrels have summoned us too late," said Waymouth to Miles Carlingford, a sigh, unheard amid the howling of the tempest, for the first time escaping his bosom. "Howbeit, we'll do what men can do to save the ship. Summon all hands with axes to clear the wreck of the masts."

In an instant every man, accustomed to the commanding voice of his chief, was actively employed. Ropes and broken spars were quickly severed, and the shattered masts and their heavy rigging were soon floating away astern. The huge foresail, which had hitherto threatened to tear the mast out of the ship, was skilfully reefed, and with somewhat diminished speed the Lion plunged onward through the foaming ocean. Still the rate at which she drove was far too great for safety, yet all had been done that could be done, and Waymouth and his followers resigned themselves like brave believing men to the rule of Him who rules the universe, and without whose will not a sparrow falls to the ground. As they tore on, the masts of a tall ship appeared ahead. Her more lofty spars and masts were snugly housed, and with the little sail she carried, evenly balanced, she rode hove to nearly head to wind. On, on drove the Lion. It was feared that she might strike the stranger. With difficulty this was avoided. People were seen on the stranger's deck, but no assistance could be expected from them. No flag flew from her peak. Her nation could not be ascertained; she might be a Hollander or a Portugal — scarcely English, from the appearance of the people and her build; certainly not one of Admiral Wood's squadron. The people on board waved and shouted, but their voices were unheard. A board was shown, but ere what was written on it could be deciphered the Lion had driven a long way by. Soon the stranger was lost to sight; no aid could be hoped for from her. On, on drove the once gallant Lion, now a helpless wreck on the waste of waters. Far from abating, the fury of the storm increased. Another damage was discovered; the wreck of the mast had struck the rudder, and now a sea carried it away. Dreadfully the battered ship labored through the foaming seas. The well was sounded. Aghast, the carpenters declared that there were seven feet of water in the hold.

"To the pumps! to the pumps!" was the cry.

The diminished crew began to labor at the pumps,

but weakened by disease they could hardly gain on the water. Buckets were employed, and those who could not work at the pumps passed them from hand to hand from below, but even thus but little progress was made in freeing the ship. All hands must work. The arch-mutineer Hagger was released from his shackles, and came to take his spell at the pumps. Without remonstrance he obeyed, though somewhat sulkily. The sick came from below, but soon sank overcome with the exertion. Others, too, who had hitherto escaped were struck by the fever. Those whom the sea had spared disease now grasped, and the numbers of the crew of the ill-fated Lion began again fearfully to diminish. Still the gale blew, and still the ship drove on. At last, the almost unknown Pacific was entered. What land would bring them up no one could tell.

They had no chart to guide — no knowledge of the unmeasured ocean across which they were driving. Thus the Lion helplessly pursued her course, the sport of the raging tempest, and vanished, as it were, into obscurity.

CHAPTER IX.

We left Antony Waymouth and his companions in misfortune on board the ill-starred Lion, which was driving at furious speed across the wide Pacific. For many days no observation had been taken, for neither sun nor stars had been visible. One compass alone remained uninjured, and that told them that their course was still easterly, and some began to assert that they would meet with no land till they struck on the vast continent of America. Would their crazy, battered bark float as long? Would their provisions and water hold out till they could reach some hospitable shore? No longer was the once docile ship under control; the rudder had been carried away, and with the scant materials at their disposal they could not construct a new one, nor while the sea ran so high could they attempt to rig it. The foresail still stood and dragged the ship forward, nor could it with safety be lowered, for without it she might have broached to, and all on board have been swept from the decks. By constant bailing and laboring at the pumps the leaks could with difficulty be kept under. Yet hope in the bosoms of Waymouth, Raymond, Ap Reece, and some of the braver spirits, was not extinct.

The more ignorant men, however, began to despair, and would, had not strict watch been kept, have broken into the spirit-room and drunk till they became unconscious of all that was occurring around.

The fever caught at Bantam had not yet left the crew, and many still lay struck down by it in their berths, while one or more continued every day to be added to the list of victims. Not a day passed that one was not carried off. No one knew who would next be called away. Seldom that more than one died in the day, yet that circumstance seemed to create greater terror than had several died together. "Who has gone to-night?" was the question asked by the survivors as each morning they met on deck after their troubled rest below. Thus gradually the crew diminished in numbers. How valueless appeared the wealth they had with so much toil and danger collected! Of the officers, Waymouth, Raymond, Carlingford, and Ap Reece, with Master Walker and the two young cabin-boys, were the only ones who had hitherto escaped. All the rest whose names have not been mentioned in this chronicle had sunk under the fell disease. Honest Dick Lizard was among the survivors, and so likewise were Hagger and Soper, and several of the mutineers. Including them, of seamen, soldiers, and idlers or landsmen not a score and a half still lived. Master Walker had not exhorted in vain, and, abashed and confounded, many of the mutineers believed that they had by their crime brought down the vengeance of Heaven on their heads.

Still Hagger and others clung to the idea of possessing the gold, and, hoping that the ship would escape foundering, waited for an opportunity to make off with it, though not knowing whither they could go. They had set their hearts on the gold, though, like the miser gloating over his hoard, they did not recollect how utterly without value it would be unless it could be exchangd for objects they might require.

For many days the storm had continued without abating. With short intervals of rest, every one on board had labored at the pumps, and the full, clear streams which flowed from the scuppers as the ship rolled from side to side showed the quantity of water which found an entrance between the planks. Now, as on she drove amidst mist and spray, dim outlines might be seen of land, or seeming land, often high as if composed of mountain-ranges, at other times low, like banks just rising above the water. Some, however, deemed the forms but those of clouds either floating high in the sky or resting on the ocean, and that could they have approached the spots where they were supposed to be, they would have vanished from the sight.

For several days no such appearances were observed; then, again, more were seen, and once more the ship drove on without a break in the circle of the horizon. At length the storm gave signs of breaking — the seas began to lessen in height, and the wind to howl less shrilly through the rigging of the remaining masts. Almost as suddenly as it had commenced, the tempest ceased, and the sea, no longer stirred by its power, went rapidly down.

Next day, as the sun rose brilliantly over the waste of waters, the wind fell altogether. Not a ripple broke the glass-like surface of the ocean; there was a perfect calm. Slowly at first the huge ship rolled from side to side, and then by degrees all movement ceased, and she lay like a log on the watery waste. No longer tossed to and fro, the planks between which the sea had found an entrance closed, and the pumps gained triumphantly on the leak. Waymouth, with his few surviving officers and friends, stood on the deck of the shattered bark; the crew lay or sat grouped about forward.

It was evident to the officers that no longer had they power to guide their ship, and it was proposed to build a boat and in her seek some island where at all events they might find food and water, and no longer be the sport of the elements.

Waymouth shook his head.

"I in no wise object, gentlemen and dear friends, to build a boat," he observed. "By her means we may guide our ship into a port; but while a plank of her holds together, I, her captain, can by no means desert her. Others may do as they judge convenient — I will not counsel; but my maxim has ever been to stay by the ship to the last."

"And I, dear friend, will stay by you!" exclaimed Raymond, stepping forward and grasping Waymouth's hand. "We are in the power of Providence, and if it is thought fit that we die on some foreign strand why should we complain? Or, if not, the means will be found by which once more we may visit our native shores."

"Well spoken and truly," said Master Walker. "I, too, will abide with our brave captain and share his fortunes."

"I never thought of doing otherwise," cried Ap Reece, "for, to say the truth, I was sure that the knaves who would have deserted him would not be worth caring for."

The two cabin-boys declared that their only wish was to remain with their brave captain.

A boat, however, must be built as the surest means of guiding the ship into a harbor or to an anchorage, and at once all hands set to work to accomplish the object. Planks, and ribs, and nails enough for the purpose were found, and all worked most diligently. There was no idleness now. No one showed greater zeal than Peter Hagger and his former associates. Waymouth, in the generosity of his heart, believed that he was desirous of making amends for his former misconduct.

The boat was of good size, so that she might, if it was required, carry all hands, either should the ship be about to sink, or be driven against rocks, or cast on shore. Masts and sails were fitted to her, and long sweeps, at each of which two men might pull. She was speedily ready, and with reason, for no one could tell at what moment she might be wanted.

"I hope that we may not want her to carry us all, for it would be a brave thing to take back the good ship, if so be we may find a harbor of refuge to refit," observed the captain as he contemplated the boat just completed.

The storm had continued long, but it seemed as if the calm was about to continue for a still longer period. Day after day the sun rose and shed a hot glare over the glass-like surface of the ocean; but there the storm-battered ship lay like a deserted wreck, scarcely capable of holding human beings, so forlorn and helpless she looked. Hopeless was the attempt to rig jury-masts, for not a spar remained of a size sufficient to bear a sail. Exertions, however, were made to build a rudder, by which, when the breeze returned, the ship might be guided free from any dangers which might appear ahead, or steered towards a promising anchorage. Materials, however, were scanty, and little expectation was entertained that it would stand any rough usage of the sea. Death, in taking away so many of the crew, had left fewer mouths to feed, and thus there appeared to be a sufficiency of provisions to last for many months, and of water there were many casks full.

Strange to narrate, the fever at length, in spite

of the calm, had quitted the ship; those who had last been taken ill were recovering, and the spirits of all somewhat revived. They expected deliverance of some sort, though they could not tell whence it might come. Some had spoken with seamen who had sailed with the famous Sir Francis Drake, and they told of beautiful islands with lofty hills, and fountains of bright waters, and groves of cocoa-nuts, and many trees with delicious fruits, and roots of various descriptions fit for food, so easy of cultivation that the happy natives lived at ease without the necessity of labor. They failed not, also, to tell of other advantages peculiarly attractive to the taste of seamen. It is not surprising that the delights offered by a life in one of these happy islands became the constant theme of conversation among the seamen, till they began to persuade themselves, that, although their gold might be of little value, they might pass their days with no small amount of contentment.

Few on board felt their situation more painfully than Edward Raymond. For the sake of one he dearly loved he had become an adventurer that he might make his fortune. He had obtained the wealth he coveted, and now it appeared that he was doomed never to enjoy it.

While the gale lasted the ship was driving onward, and might in reality be approaching home, but now she was motionless, and it seemed that thus she might remain till their food should be exhausted and all should die, and the rigging should rot, and the bulwarks and decks decay, and at length the ship herself go down into the depths of the sea. That such had been the fate of many a stout ship with her gallant crew there could be no doubt. Waymouth fully believing, however, that some island would be reached ere long where provisions and water could be obtained, had in no way stinted the crew of their usual allowance. One day, however, the carpenter desired to speak with him. His countenance, expressive of consternation, showed that something was very wrong.

"What ails it with thee?" asked the captain, concealing his own anxiety.

"An' it please your honor, the casks which I deemed full of water have leaked till not a drop in most of them remains," was the appalling answer. "We have not water for another three days."

"Bad news indeed, Master Auger, but, ere three days are over, maybe we shall reach some green island where there will be no lack of water and other things to refresh the men," answered the captain calmly. "Make not the news public, however. We must lessen the allowance, and trust that a good Providence will send us relief."

More than ever was a breeze prayed for. All on board were placed on an allowance of water sufficient only to moisten their parched tongues; yet even thus, as the calm continued, it appeared too likely that it would altogether fail. Gladly would the hapless crew have given all the gold on board the Lion for a few casks of the precious fluid. Waymouth made every effort to keep them employed. A great object was to ascertain the situation of the chief leaks; and this by perseverance he was enabled to do, as well as to stop them. By making the men constantly bathe he prevented them feeling so much as they might have done the want of fresh water; but, in spite of all his watchful care, there were some bad hearts among the crew who did not cease to plot against him. For a time, notwithstanding all their trials and hardships, the bold Gentlemen Adventurers kept up a gallant appearance; but now, at length, their sufferings began to tell upon them, and their sunken eyes, hollow cheeks, and haggard looks told plainly what they endured. No longer in brave attire with elastic step they paced the deck, but unshaven and with unarranged garments they leaned against the bulwarks, or slowly dragged their feet for a few minutes where they were wont to walk so briskly.

With longing eyes the horizon was scanned for the signs of a coming breeze. The wind came at last from the west, and once more the ship moved slowly through the water. Hope revived. For two days she continued her course, towing after her the boat which had been launched during the calm in readiness for use. Again the fitful breeze ceased, and the ship lay motionless as before. A slight breeze came, and clouds assembled, and showers fell. The grateful rain was collected in sails and buckets, and saved by every means, and afforded important relief to all remaining on board. So light was the wind that it scarce moved the heavy ship through the water. Three more days passed, and once again the ship began to move. More and more rapidly she glided along towards the east.

"America will be reached at last, friends, and then it will be hard if some Spaniard fall not in our way whom we may compel to convoy us back to Old England," observed Waymouth as he watched the progress of the ship through the water.

Once more the hearts of all on board revived; and well might they, for the sea was calm, the air pure, and the sun shone brightly from out of the blue firmament. Of provisions there were sufficient to last for some time, and the water, if husbanded with good care, might hold out till more rain should fall. The want, however, of fresh meat and vegetables began to tell, and that scourge of mariners, the scurvy, made its appearance. More than ever, therefore, did Waymouth desire to meet with some green island where his crew might refresh. The pleasant breeze continued, and wafted the ship along at moderate speed.

So limited was the number of officers that Waymouth took his watch like the rest. He had been on deck all the afternoon. Edward Raymond took the first night watch. He walked the deck thinking of home. Should he ever return there? Should he ever be united to her he loved? He believed in her truth and constancy, and until she received undoubted proof of his fate, she would not believe him lost. What a solace, what a pure delight was it to him to think of her, of her bright love, of all her noble qualities! He pitied his friend, and wished that he, too, had before he left England fixed his affections on one worthy of him. His watch at length was out, and he was relieved by Carlingford. The boatswain had appeared to be so completely contrite that he had been allowed to return to his duty, and was to have the morning watch.

Waymouth had slept longer than usual. He knew not how it was. More than once he had tried to arouse himself, and had again fallen off into slumber; while his cabin-boy had neglected to call him at the proper hour. At length he sprang up, and, dressing with the rapidity of a seaman, he hastened on deck. He gazed for a moment around with mute astonishment. No officer stood ready to receive him, not a man was to be seen on deck. The sails were lowered, and the ship lay motionless like a log upon the water. He looked astern; the boat was gone. A dreadful suspicion flashed across his mind: he was deserted. Yet could this be possible? Surely no. Raymond, his long-tried friend, the soul of honor — he would not have left him! Carlingford, the gallant seaman! Master Walker the minister, he surely was no hypocrite. Ap Reece, though hot-headed, was warm-hearted and true as steel. He shouted, again and again, "All hands on deck! all hands on deck! Your captain calls!" There was no reply. Was it fancy? A sound came forward. Before going there, he shouted once more down the after-hatchway. He had got down about half the length of the deck when Raymond's voice arrested him. He for some moments could with difficulty comprehend what had happened. He, too, had likewise only just then awoke from an unusually sound sleep. Together they hastened forward. There lay, bound and gagged, Mr. Carlingford, Dick Lizard, and several of the crew. They had all felt unusually drowsy on their watch. Suddenly they had been set upon by Hagger, Soper, and the wretches who had mutinied and been pardoned, and, before they could offer any resistance, they were all knocked down, prevented from crying out, and bound hand and foot. Several of the watch below were treated in the same manner, and without delay chests of treasure and provisions had been got up from the hold and placed in the boat, and the mutineers, leaping into her, after lowering the sails, had quitted the ship. For some time afterwards there had been a breeze, so that the sails in the boat must much have aided them in getting to a distance. Waymouth on hearing this at once suspected the whole plan of the treacherous plot which had been so successfully carried out. The mutineers had obtained some narcotic, with which he and his officers and the loyal part of the crew had been drugged, and thus the watch on deck had been easily overpowered, and allowed them time to load the boat with all they desired and to make their escape. The rest of the officers were found below, unconscious of what had happened; and Ap Reece, on awaking and examining his medicine stores, discovered that certain drugs had been abstracted which were calculated to produce sleep.

"Let the villains go. I wish them no further evil than their own deeds will assuredly produce," said the captain.

"Add, my brother, that they may be led to see the error of their ways and repent," said Master Walker. "They have souls, and those souls are precious; never let us forget that."

A theft of far greater value than that of the gold was the two casks of water, one only, partly consumed, being left.

"It behooves us to husband this with even greater care than before, though we may be thankful that we have fewer mouths to consume it," was the only remark made by the captain.

Still the truth must be said. The hearts of those left could not but burn with indignation at the treachery of their late shipmates. It was soon discovered to be even greater than at first supposed; for as soon as the sails were again set and hands were sent to the helm, it was found that the newly constructed rudder had been cut adrift, and that the ship was once more left without the means of being guided so as to escape a threatened danger or to enter a friendly port. Yet there was faith in the hearts of those brave men in God's mercy, which had preserved them hitherto so long, not in their own strength and wisdom, which they had found so utterly to fail them, and they did not despair.

Towards evening a breeze arose, and once more they were wafted onward in the same direction as before. Such means as seamen have often used were employed to guide the ship, by towing several boards, weighted at one end, astern; but they only served to keep her head in one direction. All night long they sailed calmly on. When morning broke there was a cry, "Land, land on the larboard bow!" The sun arose, the blue sea sparkled brightly, and a lovely island appeared, with yellow sand fringed by palms and numerous graceful trees and shrubs, and picturesque hills covered with wood, and waterfalls dashing down amid rocks, and pure streams flowing towards the ocean, and blue mountains rising towards the sky in the distance. The ship glided on, nearing the shore. Should she cast anchor there? A boat was seen ahead. It was their own boat, carried off by the mutineers. There was a calm spot between the rocks; the boat ran in. The ship's course would carry her clear of the land unless great efforts were made to guide her in. They watched with anxiety the proceedings of those in the boat. From amid the beautiful groves numerous bands of natives rushed out. Their skins were dark; their hair strangely dressed. They had bows and large clubs in their hands. Those in the boat made signs to show that they desired to be friendly, but the dark-skinned natives disregarded them. The seamen endeavored to shove off, but the savages, sending a thick flight of arrows, rushed into the water and seized the boat. The hapless crew in vain endeavored to defend themselves. The savages surrounded them, grappled with them, tore them from the boat with uplifted clubs, and ere many seconds had passed their brains were scattered on the sands. The remaining crew of the Lion gazed with horror on the scene. Not one of their late shipmates remained alive. Truly had retribution speedily overtaken them.

Quickly, however, the savages were seen to be launching canoes of large dimensions, each capable of containing three to five score of men. It was evident that pursuit was intended. The Lion's guns might have put them to the rout, but her powder had been well-nigh expended, and the little that remained had been greatly damaged by the water.

Had the ship been under proper government, she might, it was supposed, have run down the canoes, or, at all events, have avoided them, and not allowed them to come alongside; but as it was, there appeared great probability that the fate of the mutineers might be theirs. Still, like brave men, they felt that they had to do their best and leave the rest to Providence. Thus, with the little powder they possessed fit for use, four of the after-guns and a number of the small arms were loaded, and they continued their course. Should any reef be in the way on which it should be their fate to strike, they knew that their fate must be sealed. They could see the black savages making violent and threatening gesticulations as they labored at forcing their canoes into the water. Happily the operation was a long one. The canoes when afloat appeared even larger than on shore; they were like two large boats united by one wide deck or platform, with one mast. On this a vast sail of matting was set, and over the water they glided at a rapid rate. The warriors on board meantime were brandishing their weapons, and leaping, and dancing, and shouting. More and more canoes were launched till a whole fleet was in pursuit of the Lion, which glided on in silence as if unconscious of their presence. A fair breeze had been blowing — it began to increase. The farther the Lion got from the land the stronger it blew; the sea, too, became rougher and rougher. The canoes were closely approaching, for in the smooth water they sailed three times as fast as the Lion. Their numbers were overwhelming. Should they persevere, even the Lion's shot would avail nothing against them. Waymouth ordered that not a gun should be fired till he should give the word. On came the foe. The leading canoes were almost up to the Lion, but, no longer steady, she began to roll and pitch in the rising sea. Still eager for their prey, the savages persevered. The headmost darted alongside. The Lion's guns were depressed. "Fire, my brave men! Fire down into them!" cried Waymouth, setting the example and bringing down a savage, who, by his appearance and gestures, seemed to be a chief. Not a shot was thrown away. Some of the savages who were climbing up the ship's sides were driven back, but others, as the canoes came up, succeeded them. More and more were coming on. Just then a heavy squall struck the ship. Like a restive steed she gave a plunge forward, then rolled from side to side, shaking herself clear of the canoes surrounding her. The savages were driven from their hold; the canoes were thrown one upon the other, and on sprang the gallant Lion free from her foes. Her after-guns played upon them for a few minutes, but when, baffled and confused, they showed no signs of pursuing, the English ceased firing, and the ship pursued her course unmolested. Grateful as they were for their preservation, it was tantalizing to the crew to sail away from that seemingly lovely shore where water and the vegetables they so much needed might be procured in abundance.

"Were it not for the light of gospel truth we might be such as they are," observed Master Walker, pointing at the island. "See the earth

in that sweet spot as God hath made it, and see man in those savages as sin has made him, and as he will continue till that blessed light irradiates his mind and heart."

CHAPTER X.

The sorely-battered Lion pursued her course across the wide Pacific. The island of the black savages was soon lost sight of.

"It was the wretches' skins made them so fierce and savage," observed Dick Lizard to a messmate in the minister's hearing.

"White or black thou wilt find it the same, Dick," he remarked. "The skin is in no way to blame. It is the heart of man which is by nature so desperately wicked. Maybe we shall fall in with some white savages and find them no wise better than the black who have destroyed our late ship-mates and from whom we have escaped."

The health of the survivors of the once-gallant company of officers and men of the stout ship became worse and worse. Scarcely one but showed some signs of the dreadful disease which had attacked them. It appeared too probable that the fears of those who predicted that they and their ship would rot away in that mighty ocean — their fate unknown — would be realized. Again scarce a drop of water remained, but when the last drop was gone, clouds gathered and grateful showers gave them a supply for a few days longer.

"Were those showers sent without design?" asked Master Walker. "Surely not; let us hope on, still trusting in the Lord."

On, on they glided, sometimes becalmed if driven west, always regaining their lost ground and advancing to the east. Once more their water failed. With parched mouths they began to wish for death to end their sufferings. There was a shout from those on the lookout on deck — "Land! land!" Nearer they drew: they could not miss it. An island with hills and groves of trees; pure water must be there. Some spoke of savages to oppose their landing. As they advanced, a reef was seen over which the sea broke. Were all their hopes to be disappointed? A passage appeared through the reef, wide enough, it was hoped, for the ship to pass. Could she be taken through? Anxiously all watched her progress. A temporary steering apparatus, which in smooth water partly served the purpose of a rudder, had been rigged. It required, however, the united strength of all on board who could be spared to work it. Thus no one was idle. Raymond was stationed at the bowsprit end to watch for the appearance of sunken rocks or reefs and to give timely notice to Waymouth, who stood aft to direct the steering and to manage the sails. The land looked more and more beautiful as the Lion approached; greater would be the disappointment to the suffering mariners should they be unable to land. Before them rose the land as if just painted by the hand of Nature. There were the glittering sands, the palm-trees laden with refreshing fruit, the shady groves beneath which the cool breeze played wantonly, fertile valleys, hills of fantastic shapes covered with a rich verdure, rugged rocks projecting from their sides, and amid them sparkling waterfalls leaping downwards and sending up wreaths of snowy foam as they reached some crystal pools or rushing streamlets at their base. What rest, what quiet, what luxury might be theirs if they could but reach that lovely land! No natives were seen to impede their landing or to interrupt their enjoyment. That dreadful reef of hard coral was still before them, the sea, elsewhere so calm and blue, dashing against it with fury as if enraged at the barrier it offered to its approach. Still there was that one narrow passage clearly defined, and within they hoped to find a calm lagoon where the ship at length might be brought to an anchor if they could pass through it in safety.

The breeze increased, driving the Lion either to safety or to utter destruction. Raymond stood pointing right ahead, with his hand now diverging slightly on one side, now on the other.

"Haul away, lads, haul away!" shouted Waymouth. "Now steady! steady!"

The foam rose high on either side, curling over and falling in showers on the inside of the reef, the wind blowing it here and there, and, as the ship plunged onward amid it, almost concealing Raymond, who, however, made no sign of alarm. The ship pitched violently, the breakers roared, the foam flew around her, and then gliding on, her crew perceived that she floated in a tranquil lagoon sheltered completely from the howling gales or raging seas. A cheer burst from their throats — very different from the battle-shouts of former days which were wont to make the Portugals tremble in their shoes. The sails were furled, the anchor let go.

" Brethren, let us, as is becoming, offer our humble thanks to a merciful Heaven, which has brought us into this haven of safety," exclaimed Master Walker, and all joined heartily in the good minister's prayer.

Those were days when men were not ashamed to worship together and to acknowledge the loving Providence which guarded them from danger. Boats were lowered, and while one-half of the remnant of the once-gallant crew remained on board to guard the ship in case of surprise, the other, well armed, proceeded on shore to explore the island, and to procure, without delay, the much-longed-for fruit and water. The party in the boats, led by Waymouth, proceeded cautiously. They had had evidence of the treachery of the natives in those regions, and they every moment expected to see a band of savages rush out from among the rocks and trees to attack them. All was silent. Eagerly they stepped on shore. Waymouth posted a few men on the lookout, while the rest proceeded to knock down the cocoa-nuts and to suck out the delicious juice, not forgetting to take some to their comrades on guard. Then they hurried on to the nearest fountain, which gushed forth from the rocky side of a hill. Here filling their water-casks, they rolled them down to the boats, one of which, laden with them and cocoa-nuts, forthwith returned to the ship. Waymouth, with his small band, next proceeded to examine the island. He could scarcely believe that so lovely a spot should remain uninhabited, yet so it seemed — no sign of life, at all events, was there. The whole circuit of the island was made, and not a human being was seen. On their return, however, Ap Reece, who was exploring in a sheltered bay hitherto unvisited, shouted to Waymouth and the rest to come to him. They descended, and a spectacle met their view which told too clearly the sad history of those who had once inhabited that lovely island. Scattered about above high-water mark lay the fleshless bones of numbers of men, the spears and arrows or darts which had deprived them of life still remaining. They were warriors, for the bony fingers of some still grasped the spears or clubs with which they had in vain attempted to defend their native shore. But where were the women and children? They had undoubtedly been carried off by the conquerors. It was a melancholy scene, on which, probably, from the day of the battle no human eye had rested — no tear had been dropped for their fate. A stricter search was now instituted. Fields were observed in which roots and various plants were cultivated. On ascending the hills, in sheltered nooks, and always in some picturesque situation, habitations were discovered of curious and neat workmanship, apparently not long deserted. Ap Reece declared it as his opinion that the island was of volcanic origin, and that probably a burning mountain would be found in it. They continued their explorations, and on reaching the summit of one of the highest hills in the island they observed in the distant horizon what looked like faint blue clouds resting on the water, but which Waymouth pronounced positively to be land. It was, therefore, probable that, although the island on which they were was uninhabited, they had neighbors from whom a hostile visit might some day be expected.

"Lest they should come we must be prepared for them," said Waymouth.

"What we have seen, dear friends, proves that, lovely as is this earth, wherever man is found there a paradise does not exist," observed Master Walker. "Those who search for such a spot search in vain, believe me."

Many of those who heard Master Walker's remarks might at other times have refused to acknowledge their justice, but suffering had tamed the pride of all, and all were inclined to agree with one who had ever shown himself a true friend and counsellor. One thing was certain, that the island would afford them ample means for refreshment, and a delightful abode; the land was evidently fertile in the extreme, the scenery lovely, and the climate delicious. Having come to this conclusion, they returned on board to take the place of their comrades, who had been panting to put foot on shore.

Waymouth had a consultation with his officers, and it was agreed that their first work should be to land the guns, and stores, and freight, and to heave down the ship that her damages might be examined, and, if possible, repaired. Short-handed as they were, this was a work of time. The freight was very great, and although the mutineers had carried off much gold, still a vast quantity of immense value remained. There was gold and silver in bars and coins, and in numberless utensils, and figures, and crucifixes, and candlesticks, and there were precious stones, and silks, and spices, and all sorts of rare and rich commodities; but as their owners hoisted them with aching arms out of the hold, and conveyed them to the shore, they sighed as they thought how utterly valueless they were to them now, and how, too, probably they might never reach England, where they could be enjoyed. Huts were built in which all these valuables were stored, even before the adventurers erected habitations for themselves. Those were warlike times, and, accustomed to fighting as they were, their next care was to dig trenches and to place their guns in position, so that they might defend themselves and their property should any foes attack their island. A considerable time was consumed in these labors, though, Waymouth setting the example, the officers worked as hard as the men. Often, indeed, so unequal at first was their strength to the task they had undertaken, that even the strongest fell fainting to the ground from their exertions. Gradually, however, with the pure air and water, and the ample vegetable diet they enjoyed, they regained their health and strength, even though the rest they so much required was denied them. Having completely emptied their ship and dismantled her, even her ballast being got out, they waited till a high tide, and placed her on shore. It was with anxious eyes that they watched the carpenter as he made an examination of her hull. With auger and mallet in hand he went over every part of the ship. He then desired to speak to the captain alone. It was some time before Antony Waymouth again appeared among them.

"Friends, hear me," he said in a firm voice. "You are brave men, and will dare all that men can dare, but it is the opinion of our carpenter (and you know that his judgment is good) that our once stout ship is not in a fit condition to continue our voyage. Had we the means of repairing her we might do so, but they do not exist, and we must be content to abide our time here, or to proceed by such other means as Providence may send us."

This address of the captain was warmly received,

and his spirit appeared to be infused into theirs. Raymond probably heard the announcement with more pain than any one else. His hopes of returning home seemed forever cut off. Should he ever again see his beloved Beatrice? What probability was there of a ship visiting that island? In building the boat carried off by the mutineers they had exhausted so large a portion of the remnant of their stores that they had not sufficient to build another. One thing he was determined to do. He would cherish his love for Beatrice to the last gasp of life, and would make every effort which strength and means would afford to return to Old England. Waymouth highly applauded his resolution.

"Beshrew me, dear coz," he said, "it was a cruel wrong that I unwillingly did thee when I induced thee by my persuasions to come out to these savage regions; yet I did it for love of thee, and with good intentions, and thus I know that thou harborest no ill-will towards me in consequence. But keep up thy heart, Ned; we know not what happy turn fortune may take. Perchance, after all, we may patch up the old Lion so that she may perform the remainder of the voyage across this wide Pacific. We have well-nigh performed half of it already. Then courage, Ned, courage. Let us live on in hope."

"Thanks, dear captain. I neither blame thee nor allow hope and my heart to part company," answered Raymond. "I know not how it may happen, but still I hope to see the white cliffs of England before I die."

"So, marry, do I," exclaimed Waymouth, his own spirits rising as he talked with his friend. "We'll make the old Lion swim. There are trees for planks and spars; we must set our saws to work, and try what can be done. It may take time, but what matters that, provided we succeed in the end?"

The people generally, however, made no complaint of their lot, and as Waymouth kept them constantly employed without over-exerting them, they had no time to contemplate the future.

The most important question which arose was how they should support existence after the provisions which they had brought in the ship were exhausted. Fish might be caught, and there were roots, and fruits, and herbs which Ap Reece and Master Walker pronounced to be nutritive and good when properly cooked, but such diet would scarcely suit the stomachs and support the strength of Englishmen accustomed to the meat diet of their native land. There were no beasts on which they could feed, and the birds, which were mostly water-fowl, could only be obtained by being shot. Now although there was no want of fire-arms, nor of lead for bullets and small shot, there was only powder enough left to enable them to discharge the great guns once, or fire a few rounds of musketry. This matter caused the officers considerable concern.

Should they repair the ship or build another craft, they must have provisions, and powder for their defence and for procuring provisions; crossbows, to be sure, might be manufactured, but they were inefficient weapons compared to fire-arms, though several on board were well accustomed to their use.

There was a great probability, also, that they would be attacked some day by the natives of the islands they saw in the distance, and although victory would be certain if they could use their fire-arms, without them they might be overwhelmed by numbers and conquered. Still they went on strengthening their fort, improving their dwelling-houses, and making experiments in the cultivation of the various roots and fruit-bearing plants and shrubs they found in the island, as if they fully expected to remain, at all events, some time on the spot. They then began fashioning planks and spars for the ship, setting up a forge for the iron-work, and, as their canvas had been almost exhausted, in converting some of their rich silks — damaged, however, by the water — into sails by sewing many folded together, thus making them far stronger than any ordinary canvas. All these were works which must of necessity occupy a length of time. There was but one carpenter and one artificer who understood the blacksmith's craft. All the others had to be instructed before they could render any efficient aid, but as all were anxious for the result they labored willingly and learned rapidly.

On examining the stores which had been landed, four well-secured casks were discovered which had been taken out of one of the last prizes captured. The contents were not known till one day Ap Reece, searching for a chest of drugs, examined one of them, and pronounced them to contain saltpetre.

"Ah! that villanous drug of which Will Shakspeare speaks," exclaimed Waymouth. "To us it might be precious if combined with charcoal and sulphur; but whence is the latter to be procured?"

"We'll see; perchance it may not be so hard to find as my noble captain supposes," answered Ap Reece.

On hearing this Waymouth cheered up greatly.

"Many are the obligations we are under to you already, my good friend, and a still greater debt shall we owe to you if you discover the means of thus supplying our chief wants. Sulphur, I know, is brought home in ships from Italy, but in what other parts of the world it is found I know not," answered Waymouth, who made no profession of scientific knowledge.

"In a few days I hope to prove that I am right in my conjectures," answered the surgeon. "At all events, I pray thee have the saltpetre carefully guarded. I will set forth at break of day to-morrow in search of this article we so much covet."

When Master Walker heard of the search for sulphur, he shook his head, exclaiming —

"Alack! alack! but the other day we were all pronouncing this isle to be a paradise on earth, and now are eagerly seeking for the means of destroying life. Believe me, no paradise can exist where the shafts of death can reach."

Ap Reece was right in his conjectures. After searching for several days, he not only discovered a large amount of sulphur, but the crater of a volcano whence it had proceeded. Charcoal was next to be made, and when that was produced the surgeon commenced his preparation of gunpowder. Great was the disappointment, however, when the result appeared to be a complete failure. A black powder was produced, which burnt, but its explosive qualities were very imperfect.

Nothing daunted, however, he again set to work. Numberless experiments were made, and at length success crowned his efforts. The powder was pronounced as good as that in the small cask they had remaining. Months, however, had rolled on from the time of their first landing till the powder was produced. Though all had worked hard, the repairs of the big ship had made no great progress. Want of skill and want of tools was the cause of this. They had now, however, forged tools, and were gaining skill. Necessity truly is the mother of invention. Those who had never before handled axe or hammer were becoming fair carpenters and smiths. Sometimes as they examined the old Lion, and timber after timber and the whole lower part of the planking was found to be rotten, they were almost in despair. Some even declared that it would be useless to continue the work, till Waymouth's cheerful voice aroused them.

"Look at those noble trees, lads! Cannot they be made to produce as good timbers and planks as those that are rotten, think ye?" he exclaimed. "See the planks we have already formed! All we want is time. What we may not effect in six months we surely can in twelve. Cheer up, brave lads! cheer up!"

Such were the encouraging words he was wont to address to his men, and they had their effect. Two canoes had been formed; they were merely trunks of trees hollowed out, but they served the purpose for which they were intended — to fish from in the calm lagoons round the coast. Since a supply of powder had been obtained they were used for shooting wild fowls, whose haunts could be approached by their means on the water far more easily than by land.

Such was the state of affairs when one day Edward and Carlingford, with the two young cabin-boys, Dick Lizard, and another man, had gone out in the canoes prepared either to shoot birds or to fish. The weather being calm, and they also being on the lee side of the island, they ventured outside the reef to a greater distance than was their custom in order to visit a rock some little way off on which they expected to find an abundance of birds. They reached the rock in safety, and found not only birds but eggs in vast quantities, which would afford a healthful and pleasant change of diet. Well pleased with thus obtaining an ample supply of food with little trouble — for the eggs were to be had for the picking up, and the birds by knocking them down with sticks without firing a shot — they at once began to fill their canoes. They had well-nigh completed their cargoes, when, on looking seaward, Edward's eye fell on an object on the water seemingly approaching them. They soon discovered it to be a large double canoe. They had had proof of the treacherous nature of the savages of those regions. They soon came to the conclusion that unless they wished to engage in a sanguinary contest with the people on board the big canoe it would be wiser to return forthwith to the mainland. By the aid of their fire-arms they might undoubtedly come off victorious, but not without killing many of the savages, and this Edward was most anxious to avoid doing. All the scenes of battle and bloodshed through which he had gone had not hardened his heart, and he longed for the time when he might sheathe his sword and never draw it more.

The Englishmen took their seats in their small skiffs, and the savages in their large vessel approached the rock. They had come probably for the purpose also of collecting eggs and birds. The canoes had got about half way to the main island when they landed on the rock. They could not have been long there before they must have discovered that it had been visited, and their eyes being directed towards the island, they must have discovered the canoes.

Although the large double canoes of those seas sail at a prodigious rate when once launched, they are so heavy that they cannot with ease be pushed off from the land. Before this was accomplished the wind had risen, blowing from the island towards the rock. Edward and his companions paddled on with all their might. Their fire-arms would avail them nothing if the strangers were to attempt to run them down. It was with great satisfaction, therefore, that they saw the breeze rise, which as they drew near the shore offered no opposition to their light canoes.

"Very probably those savages are some of the people who destroyed the inhabitants of this island," said Carlingford. "They will have discovered our traces on the rock, and will fancy that some of their enemies must have escaped them."

"Whatever they think, we may expect a visit from them ere long," answered Edward. "We must be prepared for them, and as maybe there is no time for delay and we cannot afford to lose these birds and eggs, we must load ourselves with them and carry them across the island."

Drawing their canoes out of the water and concealing them in the bushes, they loaded themselves with the birds, carrying the eggs in baskets, and hurried on, leaving Mr. Carlingford to watch the proceedings of the strangers.

On receiving the information brought by Edward, Waymouth summoned his followers from all directions into the fort and made arrangements for their defence. The canoes which had pursued them must have each carried a hundred men or more, and as they did not muster altogether more than thirty souls, they could not expect without some difficulty to drive off their assailants. All their preparations were completed when the lieutenant brought word that the strange canoes had sailed away towards the land in the north-east. This incident showed them more than ever the necessity of being on their guard against surprise, and consequently lookouts were stationed on two high points in different parts of the island to give notice of the approach of any strange canoes.

Fortunate was it for the adventurers that they had a leader possessed of so much judgment and discretion as well as bravery. Some had begun to grumble at having two persons taken off every day from the important work of repairing the ship, when, ten days after the circumstance above mentioned, one of the watchmen came hurrying in to announce the appearance of a large fleet of double canoes — there might be fifteen or more, but it was difficult at the distance they were off to count them. The other lookout-man having been sent for, the first, with Lizard, went out to watch the proceedings of the strangers. Waymouth, urged by Master Walker and Raymond, resolved, if possible, to treat them as friends, and to avoid bloodshed as long as he could. One of the chief objects in building the fort was to defend the ship, and some of the guns were so placed as to play upon all approaching her.

Every possible precaution had been taken, when, in the evening, Lizard arrived, bringing the information that the enemy had landed, and appeared to be making preparations to encamp on the shore. He computed that there could not be much fewer than a thousand of them. There were no women or children; and as they were all armed, and decked out with paint and feathers, there could be no doubt that they had come with some hostile intention. Night came on, and the savages did not approach. It was possible that they might not be aware of the presence of the white men; or if they had by any means discovered the erection of the fort, they might purpose to attack it during the night. At all events, it was necessary for the adventurers to keep a vigilant watch.

The hours of darkness passed away. No foes had appeared. It was possible, however, that they might be watching in ambush in the neighborhood to rush into the fort as soon as the little garrison were off their guard. Waymouth was not a commander to be thus taken by surprise. As soon as dawn had broke he sent out scouts to examine the thickets around. No foes were there concealed;

they therefore advanced farther and farther. Gaining a height which commanded a valley along which the savages would probably approach, a party of them were seen advancing along it and examining the country on either side; some going first were evidently scouts, and tracing out the track made by the adventurers as they crossed the island. The savages were seen to halt, and they remained stationary till they were joined by a considerably larger body. The English scouts hurried back to the fort. They had not long reached it when the scouts of the enemy were seen emerging from the valley. They drew back when they caught sight of the fort, and evidently understood its object. One thing, however, it was very evident that they did not understand — the power of the guns mounted within it — for in a short time their whole army collected within range, so that it would have been in the power of the English to have destroyed a large number without giving them warning.

At Master Walker's suggestion, Waymouth, before allowing a shot to be fired, resolved to try what negotiation might effect. A white flag was hoisted in the fort, but it was totally disregarded: the savages did not understand its meaning. Several then volunteered to go out and speak to them; but as no one comprehended their language, that would be of no use. Master Walker recommended that some presents should be carried and placed on the ground midway between them. This was done;

but the savages, instead of placing others in their stead, rushing forward, carried them off with shouts of derisive laughter, taking the gifts more as a tribute than as a token of amity.

Another effort was to be made. Edward and Carlingford advanced, making signs of amity, but it seemed that they were not understood, for suddenly some hundreds of the savages, with fearful yells, rushed forward, with clubs uplifted as if to destroy them. Such evidently was their intention. Waymouth saw that there was but one way to save the lives of his friends, and he gave the order to the arquebusiers to open their fire to the right and left of the English and over their heads, while at the same time the great guns belched forth flame and shot on the advancing masses. The effect was magical. Numbers fell to the ground overpowered by fear rather than by wounds, some fled, others stood still, but none advanced. Before any had recovered from their panic, Edward and his companion were in the fort. The savages, after a short time regaining courage, collected in vast numbers on the land side of the fort, gazing with wonder at it, and at the ship, of which they could obtain a good view. The artillery had not done sufficient execution to show them its power; and once more flourishing their clubs, and leaping and shouting, they advanced towards the fort.

This was no time for trifling. Should they persevere in the face of the fire-arms, they might by their numbers alone overwhelm the little garrison. Waymouth ordered the guns to be fired this time directly at the foe. The effect exhibited when the smoke cleared off was indeed like the work of magic; the space lately filled with leaping, shouting beings was entirely emptied, except here and there a few dark forms which lay writhing or stretched at length and motionless on the ground. Not another savage was to be seen.

A shout was bursting from the lips of the adventurers at this speedy repulse of their foes, when there was a burst of flame, a terrific roar, the earth shook under their feet, earth, and rafters, and clods of grass came showering down on their heads, and the cries and groans of wounded men struck the ears of the rest with alarm. Their magazine had exploded, and every grain of powder, except such as was in the guns turned seaward and in the pouches of the arquebusiers, was destroyed. Two of their number had been killed by the explosion, and several were wounded by the falling fragments of the building. Even the bravest began to despair, and to believe that they were about to be slaughtered by the savages. The voice of Waymouth once more restored their confidence.

"What, lads! are we, who have for years past fought and conquered countless numbers of Portugals, Turks, and infidels of all sorts, to be downcast because a few casks of gunpowder blow up and a few score of naked savages are shrieking away in front of us?" he exclaimed. "Cheer up! What has happened is but the fortune of war. Probably the savages, having had a specimen of our prowess, will not venture again to molest us, and if they do we have still some powder and sharp swords with which to defend ourselves."

These words had the effect intended. Ap Reece attended to the wounded. The two poor fellows who had been killed bringing out the powder were buried, and the adventurers waited with calmness for the return of the savages, should they again venture on an attack. Waymouth was certain that they still remained in the neighborhood, as now and then a person could be seen passing in the far distance, and he was loath to send out a scout lest he might be set on by any natives lying in ambush and carried off.

Darkness returned. Strict watch was kept, and few of the adventurers closed their eyes in sleep. Long and dreary seemed the night. Would the savages pluck up courage and return to the attack? If they were of the same character as those who had destroyed the mutineers, more ferocious savages it would be hard to find. Sounds were heard during the night, but the stars were obscured by clouds and mist, and no object could be discerned at any distance from the fort.

Morning at length returned, and by the light of day it was discovered that both the dead and the wounded had been carried off. It was important to ascertain whether the enemy still lurked in the neighborhood. Several of the party volunteered to go out for this object. Waymouth accepted the offer of Carlingford and young Martin. Their progress was anxiously watched from the fort. They at length disappeared among the trees. Their friends trembled lest the savages might set on them. Now two objects were seen moving on a hill in the distance: it might be them. Two hours passed away. They did not appear. Either the enemy having taken their departure, they had proceeded across the island, or they had been set upon and destroyed. Several wished to go out to search for their friends, but this Waymouth would not allow. Their fears were, however, banished when their lost friends were seen approaching. They brought the intelligence that the savages had embarked in their large canoes and had sailed away. This was satisfactory news.

In vain, however, did they endeavor to manufacture some powder instead of that which had been destroyed. Without saltpetre they could do nothing. For some time, also, they could make no progress with the ship. The carpenter and smith had both been injured by the explosion, and the two men killed had been among the best artificers. Often as Waymouth and Edward examined the work, they agreed that it might have been wiser to have built a new vessel altogether of much smaller dimensions. Still, notwithstanding all their disappointments

and difficulties, they proved themselves to be true men by perseveringly laboring on. One error was allowed to be committed. When all fears of the return of the savages had subsided, the desire to obtain birds was so great that the powder was expended to shoot them, those on the rock having been mostly frightened away. Many more months passed away. Had it not been for good Master Walker, who ever reminded them of the Sabbath, and exhorted them on that day to refrain from work, they would have lost all note of time.

The hull was at length almost completed; the sails were manufactured, and a supply of cordage; the masts had next to be formed and got in, as also the spars. The larger trees best suited for the purpose were on the opposite side of the island, and a party had gone across to select some for the purpose required, when, after a time, they were seen hurrying back with looks of consternation. They had cause for alarm. A fleet of canoes twice as numerous as that of their former visitors was seen approaching the island, and would soon be on shore. Signals were made to recall all those at a distance into the fort. Every means which could be thought of was taken to strengthen the fortifications. An examination was made of the remaining powder. The error which had been committed was evident; there was not enough to load all the great guns, leaving none for the smaller pieces, and of that little which remained a considerable portion was damp, and would require to be dried before it could be used.

Waymouth, in this emergency, endeavored as before to inspire his followers with courage. He ordered three guns to be loaded pointing in the direction by which it was expected the savages would approach if their purpose was to attack the fort. The rest was divided among the arquebusiers, who were charged not to throw a shot away. There were a few crossbows which were eagerly brought into requisition, and every man had besides a pike, battle-axe, and sword, so that, compared to the savages, they were well armed. Still it was fearful odds for eight and twenty men to contend against a thousand. The night was approaching. The sun went down in an angry mood, and the wind began to blow strongly, and went on increasing till it raged fearfully among the tall palm-trees, which bent like willow wands before its fury. Fiercer and fiercer it blew.

Sentinels were posted round the fort, for it was conjectured that the savages might make their approach during the darkness, in the hopes of taking the garrison by surprise. The gray dawn appeared. No foe was in sight. Just, however, before the sun should arise — for his beams could not penetrate through the dark canopy of clouds overhead — suddenly from every quarter on the land side appeared from among the trees large bodies of savages dressed with their war ornaments, and wildly flourishing their weapons, while, as they rushed on, they uttered the most fearful shrieks. Nearer they approached. At a signal from Waymouth the guns opened on them; but though many were laid low, this did not stop the rest. The guns no longer roared. The foe came on as before; like ants they swarmed round the fort. The arquebusiers reserved their fire till the enemy was close upon them. Now began the fierce strife. As the savages rushed on they were driven back with the bullets which hailed on them, with thrusts of pikes and blows of battle-axes. Still more came on. These were no ordinary savages. It was evident that they were well accustomed to scenes of bloodshed: they fought more like demons than men. They were driven back only to return with greater fury, like the waves of the stormy ocean.

Three of the adventurers lay dead, several more were wounded; still the brave band encouraged each other to persevere. They mostly fought with desperation, not expecting to escape, but resolved to sell their lives dearly. More savages were coming on, when suddenly they paused. Those who were fighting drew back with astonishment in their countenances. Waymouth, who was everywhere, rushing here and there to aid those the most hard pressed, turned his eyes seaward, and there he beheld a fine ship with her tacks aboard, endeavoring to beat off the island, which it was evident she had discovered at daybreak, when too late, close under her lee. She might escape the most dangerous reef, but there was a point of land on which he judged that she must inevitably strike. All the canvas she could carry was set, and heeling over to the gale she plunged furiously through the foaming seas. He shuddered to think what would be the fate of her crew should they fall into the hands of the savages, and he longed to be able to hurry to their assistance. The savages, meantime, it seemed, believed that she was some being sent to the assistance of those with whom they were fighting, and, calling loudly to each other, they sprang back out of the conflict, and the whole body rushed away into the cocoa-nut grove, and were soon hid from view.

CHAPTER XI.

Beatrice Willoughby was seated, with her embroidery before her, in the withdrawing-room of the old hall where her childhood's happier days had been passed. Her dress showed that she had lost some near relative. In truth, the Lady Willoughby, her mother, had been summoned to happier realms, and she and Hugh were left orphans, alone in the world, all in all to each other. Hugh had altered much for the better. He felt his responsibilities — that his dear sister was greatly dependent on him — and her happiness had become his chief care. She was not, however, dependent for support on him, for she had a handsome dower, which would enable her to live as became her rank. She was not alone; Hugh was there, seated at a window, engrossed in a book of travels, for to see the wide world had become the great desire of his heart. Unable himself to wander forth to foreign lands, he obtained every book in his power which described distant countries and the adventures of those who had visited them.

Beatrice had a more sociable companion than her brother in sweet Constance Raymond, who, having lost the old knight her father, had lately taken up her abode with her friend. Both girls were mistresses of themselves, and enjoyed no small satisfaction in feeling their independence. Hugh no longer affected Mistress Constance. He had been so long in her company that he had learned to look on her in the light of a sister whom it was his duty to protect and support as he felt that he should his own sister Beatrice. In truth, sweet Mistress Constance, being a year or more older than Hugh, and of a somewhat vehement if not imperious temper, had herself done much to cure him of the tender sentiment which at one time seemed about to spring up in his bosom.

The young people were not, however, without one who acted the part of a guardian, although he could not claim the legal right of being so. This was honest John Langton — Captain John Langton — a devoted friend and follower of their honored father, Sir Hugh Willoughby. Sickness had prevented him from going that fatal voyage from which the brave knight never returned. Captain Langton was an experienced seaman; he had made many voyages to various regions, and was a man of great judgment and discretion. Although the snow of the winter of life had already sprinkled his head, his health and strength were unimpaired, while the spirit of adventure which had tempted him abroad in his younger days lay smouldering within his bosom, ready to burn up should occasion blow upon it. He lived in a small mansion close by the hall, where he was an almost daily visitor.

It may be supposed that the very constant subject of conversation between the two young maidens was the fate of him who had been so long absent, and of whom since they had last received tidings more than two years had passed — long, long years they had been to them. Still they lived on in hope of hearing of Edward, or some day of seeing him walk in, full of health and strength, and to hear him recount the adventures he had gone through. As to the wealth he had coveted, it mattered little to them whether he brought it or not, provided he was never again tempted to go in search of it. There was another, too, in whose fate, though he knew not of it, the lovely Constance was interested. When Edward had written home he had spoken little of his own deeds, but he had enlarged greatly on the gallantry of his friend Waymouth, and her enthusiastic imagination adding lustre to his acts, she had pictured him to herself as worthy of being a hero of romance, and had without hesitation encouraged that sentiment towards him, which, if not love, was nearly allied to it.

Hugh, who had come to the end of his book, and was gazing out of the window, wondering when he should have the opportunity of visiting the scenes described therein, suddenly exclaimed —

"There is a stranger coming along the paths. His dress, much the worse for wear, betokens him to be a seafaring man, and his features are dark and weather-beaten. Maybe he brings tidings from the distant Eastern seas."

The hearts of his fair hearers beat quick as they heard these words. Who could this weather-beaten stranger be? They in the same breath entreated Hugh to hasten out and to bring in the seaman lest he should pass by, not that it was likely he would so do without stopping to ask an alms or the means of proceeding on his way. He was evidently foot-sore and weary, and probably hungry and poor, and as such alone claimed their compassion. Hugh gladly hurried out, and soon returned with the wayfarer. He was a man of middle age, and, though his countenance spoke of toil and torrid climes, he was stout of limb and broad of shoulder, and had no lack of work in him; and, though his garments were worn almost to tatters, they had once been of a rich description. He doffed his battered beaver as he entered the hall, and stood before the fair dames in a humble posture, waiting till they addressed him.

"Whence come you, stranger, and what brings you into these parts?" asked Beatrice in a gentle voice calculated to give encouragement to the person she addressed.

She spoke not without hesitation, and in truth she had no great expectation of hearing aught of him she loved.

"I come, lady, from far-distant regions; my calling is on the sea, my birthplace near Gloucester; and landing at Plymouth without rhino in my purse, food in my pouch, or friends to afford me any, I have been working my way as best I could to that home where I hope to find rest and quiet after all my toils," answered the stranger bluntly.

"What took you to those foreign lands?" asked Beatrice, somewhat disappointed with the answer.

"My own folly, and, maybe, greed of gain," he replied in the same tone. "I gained wisdom, and might have gained wealth had it not taken to itself wings and flown away."

But with whom did you sail to those far-distant realms? Surely you went not alone?" said Constance in a tone which showed that she might not be inclined to brook a saucy answer.

"Your pardon, fair ladies; I saw not the drift of your questions," replied the seaman. "I sailed in the company of a brave admiral, Captain Lancaster, on board his tall ship the Red Dragon, with several other goodly ships, the Serpent, the Lion, the Lion's Whelp"—

"Can you give us tidings of any on board the Lion?" exclaimed Beatrice, eagerly interrupting him.

The stranger shook his head.

"Bad tidings only, I fear, sweet ladies," he answered with some feeling. "Of all that gallant company, captains, and officers, and men, I am the only one, to the best of my belief, who yet breathes the air of heaven — except," he added, seeing the effect his words were producing on his fair auditors, "one of the ships, storm-driven, found a haven of which I know nothing; the remainder of the brave squadron I saw go down into the ocean depths with all their gallant crews" —

"What — what was the name of the ship which may have escaped that dreadful doom?" exclaimed both the fair girls at once in accents scarcely articulate from agitation.

"The Lion was the ship, once commanded by Captain Wood, and, when he became admiral, by Captain Antony Waymouth, as brave an officer as ever held a sword," answered the seaman, evidently now wishing to speak to the purpose. "We had long been parted from him, I being still on board the Red Dragon, when a fierce tempest arose — so fierce I had never before encountered. One by one we saw consorts, long battered by the waves and shattered in battles innumerable, go down, all on board perishing. Scarcely could the Red Dragon keep afloat, much less render assistance to others. Her turn came. We had been driving to the east, hoping to find a haven where we might repair our damages, when, even in sight of land, the tempest still raging, a whole plank, it seemed, started, for, without many minutes for preparation, the big ship began to settle bodily down into the sea. There was no time to cut loose the boats — no time to form a raft. I felt the deck sink under me; shrieks and cries arose. I clutched a large spar which had been left unsecured on deck, and found myself floating amid the foaming waves. My companions in misfortune gradually disappeared. One by one they sank down till I was alone. The storm subsided. For nearly two days I clung to the spar, and when my strength was well-nigh gone, a ship of the Hollanders, sailing from land, took me aboard. The gale had but sunk to rest for a season. It rose again, and the stout ship was driven before it far to the east amid islands with which no one on board was acquainted. We explored among them for a long time, but the hurricane season was not over. Our captain observed signs of a coming storm, and with a sagacity for which those Hollanders are justly famed he brought up inside a reef, where, sheltered from the sea, we might lie safely at anchor. While there, the gale continuing, I saw a ship approaching, and feared greatly that she might be dashed on the reef. Anxiously I watched her as she drew near. I knew her at once, having so long sailed in her company. She was the once tall ship the Lion, now sadly shattered and shorn of her beauty. She escaped the reef but by half a cable's length, it seemed, and on she drove to the westward. As long as I could see her from the mast-head, to which I ascended, escaping all dangers, she drove in the same direction. Scarcely could I hope, however, with the numberless islands which besprinkle 'that ocean, she could drive clear of them all. Still she may have escaped. The gale continued for many days. Sometimes the wind dropped, but the skipper refused to leave the shelter of the reef, and sure enough before long the storm raged again more furiously than ever. It was his opinion, too, that the gale would continue blowing on towards the east, so that a ship might be driven half round the world by it before she would again find herself in a calm. But I weary you, fair ladies."

"Go on, go on, good friend!" exclaimed Beatrice, her bosom heaving with agitation. "Didst ever gain further tidings of the Lion?"

"No, lady, not from that day to this," answered the seaman. "All I know is that it was the Hollander's opinion if any of her company survive they must be dwelling on one of the islands of the Pacific, on whose shore, undoubtedly, the ribs of the good ship are lying."

"Beatrice! Hugh! let us go and search for them!" exclaimed Constance, springing up with her eyes streaming, and her hands clasped in an appealing attitude, first turning to one and then to the other. "Stranger, could you guide a ship in the direction in which you think they were driven? We would search every shore, we would visit every island in that mighty Pacific, till we found them. It were a shame if we were to allow my noble brother Edward and that gallant Captain Antony Waymouth to perish on some desert isle without making an effort to save them, and bring them back to their native shores. Hugh, the credit of your manhood is at stake an' you decline to help us, and I know Beatrice too well to doubt that she will bear me company, and go I will round and round the world if I can find men to man the ship."

"I promise you, sweet coz, that if you go I will bear you company, and I will answer for brother Hugh," said Beatrice, taking her friend's hand. "I would, however, that good Master John Langton could have a word with this stranger; he would understand far more of his account than, with our small knowledge of sea affairs, we can do. What is thy name, friend? We will ask Captain Langton to come up to the hall to see thee."

The seaman looked somewhat puzzled as he replied —

"I am known, lady, as simple Josiah Weedon, and I will gladly talk with Master Langton, but I have an aged mother and sister, and a wife who was sorely displeased at my leaving her before, and I doubt that she will let me quit home again; yet to please two such sweet ladies as you are, and to bring back to the world two such gallant gentlemen as Captain Antony Waymouth, and his lieutenant Master Edward Raymond, I would again risk the dangers of the sea and part from my loving spouse, provided we were simply to make the voyage out and home, spending some fixed time in the search."

"Thanks, Master Weedon, thanks!" exclaimed Constance enthusiastically; "we would join our prayers with yours to persuade your wife to let you come, if that would avail."

"My better-half, ladies, is one woman in a thousand. If she will, she will, you may depend on't; if she won't, she won't, and there's an end on't. I will hie me home, and should she consent I will send you word; if not, you will know that I am kept bound in the chains of matrimony."

Suddenly Hugh recollected that probably the stranger was hungry, which he confessed to be the case. Refreshment was therefore placed for him in the dining-hall, to which he set himself to do ample justice, and while he was discussing it Beatrice sent a messenger to summon Master Langton. The old captain soon appeared. His astonishment at hearing the account given by Weedon was very great, but far greater was it on hearing of the resolution to which his fair friends had so suddenly arrived. He knew Constance too well by this time to attempt to combat it. Before he made any remark, however, he had a long conversation with the stranger. He seemed perfectly satisfied that he was honest and his statements true, though he doubted much the likelihood of the missing ship being found. It was not a matter to be settled in a hurry; much discussion would be required, and he could not find it in his heart to oppose the scheme altogether.

Pressed by Hugh, Master Weedon gladly consented to remain that night at the hall to rest, and if he ate and drank abundantly he deserved his provender in return for the way he plied his tongue for Hugh's benefit. Hugh would scarcely have allowed him to sleep had he not cried out that his tongue could wag no more. Next morning, while discussing the ale and beef and wheaten bread placed before him at breakfast, he was compelled by the young man to begin again, and before he was permitted to go on his way he had given Hugh a large amount of information about those eastern seas and strange lands among which he had so long wandered. The ladies had filled a satchel with good food, and pressed on the seaman a purse with a store of coin to enable him with ease to reach his journey's end. There was little doubt that the subject would be discussed by the two maidens and Hugh. In truth, morning, noon, and even, it was the only matter about which they could speak; even Captain Langton caught much of their enthusiasm. Hugh was fully as warm as his sister or Constance. Means would not be wanting between them to fit out a tall ship able to sail round the world. John Langton must be captain; they would take no refusal. Master Josiah Weedon should be pilot if his wife would let him go, and if not, no doubt he could give such directions to Captain Langton as would enable him to sail in the direction they desired, where they might perchance discover the Lion. At length their importunity, if not their reasoning, succeeded in overcoming all Master Langton's scruples, and he consented to search for a suitable ship, to fit her out and store her, and to find the necessary officers and crew. Not many days had elapsed, and just as Captain Langton was about to set off for Plymouth, when Josiah Weedon arrived habited exactly as before.

"Fair ladies, Master Hugh, I am ready to sail with you to any part of the world you may desire," he exclaimed as he entered the house. "Things are changed since I left home, and beshrew me I was an idiot to expect it to be otherwise. My good old mother is in her grave; had she been alive I should have had a different tale to tell. My sister is married and gone far away I know not whither, and my wife, why she has gone away with my sister and a new husband of her own into the bargain, and not a soul in the place would acknowledge me. My doublet is threadbare and tattered. Josiah Weedon was always the best-dressed man in the village. I was a wretched beggar. Josiah Weedon was to come back with a dozen packhorses laden with gold and precious stones. Many more bitter remarks were made, and finally I was kicked out of the village as a rogue and vagabond, and glad enough to hurry back that I may lay my sword and services at your feet, fair ladies, right willing to do your behests in any way you may command me."

The young people did not doubt the truth of Master Weedon's story, and, after he had fed, Hugh hurried him off to Captain Langton that he might accompany him the next morning to Plymouth.

While the captain and pilot were selecting a ship and fitting her out, Hugh, with his sister and Constance, was engaged with those learned in the law in arranging for the necessary funds and the disposal of their estates, should they not live to return to the shores of Old England. Yet so sanguine is youth that not one of them ever for a moment believed that they should not return successful. Hugh was the least likely to be disappointed; he would, at all events, see much of the world, and would meet with many adventures. He forgot that it is possible to meet with disagreeable as well as agreeable adventures.

Before long Captain Langton wrote word that he had purchased a stout ship, which Constance insisted should be called the Esperanza, or Hope. Captain Langton was well known, and he had little difficulty in selecting a goodly company, especially when the object of the voyage was understood. Many young gallants offered their services on hearing that Mistress Beatrice Willoughby and Mistress Constance Raymond were themselves going on it, and were much disappointed on having them courteously refused. Captain Langton selected as his officers staid, steady, and trusty men, who were likely to keep one object in view — their duty — and not to depart from it.

The tall ship Esperanza, with banners and streamers flying and the white canvas spread to the breeze, sailed down Plymouth Sound on her way to the far-off lands of the East. Never ship bare richer freight, for never sailed over the salt seas two fairer damsels with more loving, faithful hearts. Fair blew the breeze, calm was the sea, just rippled by the joyous wind, and bright the sky overhead. Even John Langton caught some of the enthusiasm of his young charges, and could not help predicting a favorable termination to the adventure. Well was the good ship called the Esperanza, for all on board felt hope reigning in their bosoms except Master Weedon, the pilot. When rallied on his gravity he replied—

"I prithee do not ask me to rejoice at the prospect of the future who have been oft so cruelly deceived. If matters turn out well, good; it will be time enough to rejoice then; if ill, it will be but as I expect. I shall at least have the satisfaction of knowing that I have not laughed in vain. Meantime I will do my duty, and guide the ship towards those regions where the fair dames and their brother desire to proceed. May their star be a happier one than mine!"

This was the usual style of Weedon's remarks. Inside a rough shell there was a tender heart, which had been sorely wounded by the reception he had encountered on his return to the place of his birth.

Hugh Willoughby, on the contrary, was full of life and animation. Every thing he saw was new and strange, and afforded him delight, and he looked forward without doubt to the complete success of their enterprise. The ship sailed on without interruption till the burning rays of the sun, which shone down on the deck, making the pitch to bubble up out of the seams, and driving the ladies to seek the shadow of the sails, warned them that they were already in southern latitudes. The elder seamen laughed at the notion of the weather being hot.

"Do you call this hot?" said Master Weedon. "Why, good friends, we were wont during calms in those eastern seas to cook our victuals on the bare planks or on a sheet of tin placed on the deck. I can certify that we shall have it far hotter than this."

The breeze still held fair, though coming off the land of Africa, said to lie some twenty leagues away on the larboard beam.

"A sail! a sail!" was shouted by the seaman on the watch in the top. "To the eastward, and seemingly approaching us," he replied to the questions put to him.

Mariners sailing over the ocean in those days had to be on their guard against foes in every direction. Every preparation was made to give the stranger a warm reception should he prove an enemy. The heavy guns and all fire-arms were loaded; battle-axes, pikes were got up, and placed with slow matches in readiness for use; swords were girded on, and the deck of the Esperanza — generally so quiet and peaceful — assumed a thoroughly warlike appearance.

When all things were ready, Hugh approached the ladies.

"Fair friend and sweet sister, I am about to exert some little authority over you," he said. "Should yonder stranger prove to be a foe, you must descend into the hold, where you will be free from danger. When we have driven off, or captured, or sunk the enemy, we will summon you from your prison-house to rejoice with us in our victory, and to reward those who have exhibited most valor in the fight."

To this arrangement neither Beatrice nor Constance showed any inclination to agree.

"But suppose one of the foeman's shot was to deprive you of life," argued Hugh. "In battle, methinks, bullets pay little respect to persons."

"We shall but die in the performance of our duty and in the execution of our mission," answered Constance.

Hugh, not quite comprehending her remark, observed —

"Yes; but one might die, and one might escape — and alack for the survivor!"

Still the ladies insisted on remaining.

"Take your will, take your will, fair ladies. I would not quarrel with you at such a time," he said in a mournful tone. "But I pray that neither of you may be killed, though, perchance, a bullet may tear open that fair cheek, or a splinter may deprive sweet Beatrice of an eye. Although I doubt not Edward's love would stand the test, it would be a sorry plight in which to greet him should we haply discover the land where the Lion is cast away."

The fair damsels looked at each other.

"Brother Hugh, we will follow your counsel and seek shelter in the hold, where we may offer up prayers for your safety," said Beatrice humbly, Constance signifying, at the same time, that she agreed with her friend.

The stranger approached. A crescent was seen on her green ensign. She was undoubtedly a Sallee Rover. They were in the latitude where those vultures of the ocean were wont to cruise. Hugh hurried the ladies below. The ports of the Esperanza were closed, and many of the crew hidden away under the bulwarks, so that she looked but little able to defend herself. Not that any ship in those days went to sea unarmed — as well might a lamb attempt to sport among a troop of hungry lions. The Sallee Rover approached, with her infidel banners flying, her brazen trumpets braying, and her deck covered with turbaned swarthy Moors, expecting to obtain an easy victory.

John Langton kept his good ship on her course without replying. He well knew that, should victory not be obtained, the alternative must be death, or — worse than death — a life-long slavery. Not a man on board but resolved to triumph or to go down fighting for his own sake, but much more for the sake of the fair ladies he had sworn to serve and protect.

Louder blew the trumpets of the Moors as their ship came within shot of the Esperanza. Nearer and nearer they drew. Their purpose, it seemed, was to run the English ship on board, and to overcome her crew by superior numbers. Captain Langton watched for the best moment to fire. Already the dark-skinned infidels stood, with their cimeters in hand, crowding the side, and some in the rigging, ready to spring on board.

"Raise the ports, and give it them!" shouted the brave English captain.

His gallant crew cheerfully obeyed, and the next instant twenty Moors were seen struggling or dead, prostrate on the deck of the Rover, which made a vain attempt to haul her tack aboard and sheer off. Again the English crew loaded their guns ready to fire, as with a crash she ran alongside. This time they were pointed at her hull, and fearful was the execution they caused. Many of the Moors endeavored to spring on the deck of the Esperanza, but they were driven headlong back with pikes and battle-axes, too late to regain their ship, which broke clear of the Englishman, and they fell headlong into the sea. Then fearful shrieks arose as the Esperanza sailed on — the Sallee Rover was sinking. Was mercy to be shown to those who never showed it to others? The choice was not allowed them.

Before the canvas could be taken off the English ship, the Rover had sunk beneath the sea, and not a Moor remained struggling on the surface.

Beatrice and Constance, finding that the firing and turmoil of battle had ceased, entreated that they might come on deck. They gazed around in astonishment on every side; no foe was there; and except a few of the crew with limbs bound up, and here and there the white splinters where the shot from the Rover had struck the bulwarks, not a vestige of the fight was to be seen. Even then the eyes of most on board were gazing at the spot where the Rover had gone down, as if they expected to see her emerge again from her watery grave. The damsels could scarcely believe their senses.

"Heaven has fought for us," said Captain Langton. "We did our duty, but no power of ours could have accomplished what has been done. I pray that it may prove the first of many successes leading to that which may crown our hopes."

"I pray so too, kind friend," answered Beatrice, her eyes filling with tears as she thought of the danger from which they had been preserved.

Such was the tone of feeling of the voyagers — ay, and of many of the boldest adventurers — of those days. They gave Heaven the praise for all their deliverances and successes, and threw the blame when they failed on their own folly and neglect. There were clear-sighted, right-judging, and truly pious men in those days, who were laying the foundation of England's glory and power. The age which produced a Shakspeare produced many other gigantic intellects and true men.

The Esperanza sailed on, hope swelling the hearts of her owners and a fair wind her canvas, till Afric's southern cape, known by the name she bore, that of Bona Esperanza, appeared in sight.

Master Weedon counselled that they should not enter Table Bay, but proceed on to Saldanha Bay as more convenient for watering, and where they were less likely to receive interruption. As they drew near two tall ships were seen at anchor. They might be foes more likely than friends, where foes were so numerous and friends so few. The captain seemed doubtful whether it were wise to enter.

"We may fight them if they oppose us, and conquer them as we did the Rover," cried Hugh. "Maybe when they know our errand, whatever their nation, they may be inclined to aid us."

Master Weedon seemed rather doubtful of this, but Captain Langton sided with Hugh, and the Esperanza was accordingly steered towards the bay, running up a white flag as a signal of truce at the fore. It was well that this precaution was taken, for the strangers proved to be two Hollanders, always jealous of the English who appeared in those parts. The captains, however, when they found that their trade was not to be interfered with, and that there were two fair ladies on board the Esperanza, proved themselves to be honorable and courteous gentlemen. They begged permission to visit the English ship, and offered all the aid in their power to forward the object of the adventurers.

This aid was gratefully accepted, and picked men from their crews being sent by them the rigging of the Esperanza was quickly set up, and other repairs effected, and wood and water got on board, so that she was able to sail to the east in their company. Scarcely were the three ships out of sight of land when several sail were espied coming from the west. The Hollanders hailed to notify that they must be part of a Portugal fleet which they had reason to expect ere long in those seas. Should the Portugals espy them they would assuredly make chase and not spare either ships or crews should they come off victorious. As more strange ships were seen coming up, flight was their only prudent course. All sail was made, accordingly, to escape. The strangers had espied them, for they also crowded on canvas in pursuit. Captain Langton informed the Hollanders that no English fleet had of late sailed with so many ships as now appeared.

"Then they are Portugals, and we must escape them if we value our lives or liberty," was the answer.

Though the Hollanders were stout ships, yet the Portugals had faster keels, it seemed, for in spite of the wide spread of canvas set by the former they gained rapidly on them. The Esperanza might have gone far ahead; and though the Hollanders hailed and begged Captain Langton so to do, he replied that it went against his stomach to do such an act — to desert those who had befriended him. Hugh applauded his resolution, and Beatrice and Constance agreed with him. The Esperanza therefore shortened sail that she might not run away from her heavier-sailing consorts. They insisted, however, that she should keep a short distance ahead, that they might bear the first onslaught.

There was ample time to make every preparation for the fight, and the shades of evening were coming on before the leading ships of the Portugals got up with the stout Hollanders. It was now to be seen whether to sail fast or to fight stoutly were of most avail. So fiercely did the Hollanders receive their assailants that the first three of them dropped astern in confusion; others coming up were treated in the same manner. Hugh was so delighted with the bravery of the Hollanders that he begged Captain Langton to drop astern into the fight.

"No, no, the post of honor is the station assigned to them," answered the captain. "Should any of the Portugals pass our friends it will then be our duty to fight them. Let us not wish to deprive the brave Hollanders of the glory they are winning for themselves."

CHAPTER XII.

The Hollanders sailed steadily on: the wind freshened. Still more of the Portugal ships were coming up: the three friends held steadily on their way. The Hollanders sent heavy shot from their sterns, sorely discomposing their pursuers. The wind, too, was increasing, and clouds were gathering, and darkness coming on. It was clear that the Portugals were being drawn away from their intended port. This encouraged the Hollanders to hold out; yet they contended against fearful odds. Now the whole Portugal fleet, crowding on still more sail, pressed up to overwhelm them. It would have been wiser of the said Portugals had they allowed their expected prey to pass on their way unmolested. A terrific blast struck their ships, rending sails and snapping spars and topmasts in every direction, and throwing the whole fleet into confusion; while the stout Hollanders, with their stronger canvas, glided calmly on, uninjured by the gale, though sorely battered by the shot of the enemy. Darkness speedily came on, and shut out their foes from their sight. When morning broke, not an enemy's ship was to be seen. Captain Langton hailed the Hollanders gratefully to acknowledge the gallant protection they had afforded the Esperanza; whereon the two captains appeared, and, waving their hats, assured him that it was their delight and pleasure to serve ladies as fair and excellent as those who sailed on board her. The heavy sea running prevented any further communication for some days. Thus escorted, the Esperanza sailed on towards Batavia; whence it was proposed that she should take fresh departure towards the little-known seas to the east, whither the Lion had been seen driving. Space will not allow an account of all the attentions paid to Beatrice and Constance at Batavia, and the magnificent *fête* which the governor gave in their honor; for, even in those good old days, fair ladies were not often found sailing round the world in search of lost lovers and brothers, albeit the so doing was a most praiseworthy and commendable act. Certes, few damsels would be so confident as were these two heroines, that, should they succeed in their search, the brothers or lovers would be ready to exhibit that amount of gratitude which Beatrice and Constance looked for as their reward. It was reported that Constance, who was known only to be looking for her brother, received and refused uncounted offers of marriage from the governor, as well as from all the chief unmarried officers of the colony who could aspire to that honor, and that she was entreated to reconsider the subject, and to return to their fair port; while Beatrice was assured, with all the delicacy of which the mind and language of a Hollander is capable, that, should she not succeed in her search, it would be entirely her own fault should she remain long in single blessedness.

Happily, the sickly season had not commenced at Batavia, before the Esperanza was once more ready for sea; and thus the adventurers escaped the fate which has overtaken so many voyagers who have visited those sickness-causing shores. The governor and all the chief officers accompanied the ladies to their boat; the whole population gathered to see them embark; handkerchiefs waved, shouts arose, prayers for their safety were uttered; and the guns from the forts and all the shipping in the harbor fired as the anchor of the Esperanza was won from its oozy bed, and, the sails being spread, she glided forth on her perilous way.

It was reported that the governor and several of his officers shed tears as they thought of all the numberless dangers to which those fair dames would be exposed; but on that point the author of this faithful chronicle feels some doubt, for reasons which he does not consider right to disclose.

The fair damsels themselves felt few alarms or doubts: they were grateful for all the kindness they had received, and still more thankful that they had escaped from the place, and were once more on the free ocean. They had no longer cause to dread interruption from Portugals or from the ships of other civilized nations. The Governor of Batavia had given them letters charging all true Hollanders to render them every assistance in their power, and they hoped by watchfulness and prudence to escape from the hands of the savage people inhabiting the countries towards which they were sailing. They were well supplied with provisions and ammunition, and hoped that they might be delayed in no place, except to make the necessary inquiries for the Lion, and to take in water and wood; for, albeit heroines are described in romances as performing long journeys without food or shelter, ships cannot sail over the ocean without stopping to take in fresh supplies of water that their crews may drink, and wood with which to cook their victuals.

As yet, not a word respecting the Lion or her possible fate had they heard. Still their spirits did not flag while they approached the spot where Master Weedon had last beheld her. Seamen were stationed in the tops to keep a lookout for any strange sail, or for islands where the information they sought might be obtained. Again want of space prevents a description of the many places at which they touched, and the strange people they beheld. The Esperanza held her course to the east, skilfully navigated, and escaping many dangers. Right well and faithfully did Master Weedon fulfil his engagement: he pointed out the very reef within which the Hollander had taken shelter when he had seen the Lion drive by.

"Henceforward," he concluded, "I will submit to the superior knowledge of Captain Langton in the guidance of our good ship."

Due east the Esperanza now sailed. Mariners in those days troubled not their heads about circular storms or any such theories; and therefore it was concluded, that if a gale was blowing from the west, before which the Lion was driven, she most assuredly would be found to the east. Now on one hand, now on the other, islands were espied and visited; but no information was obtained. Either there were no natives, or they fled at the approach of the strange ship; or, when natives were found, no means existed of exchanging ideas between the voyagers and them.

At length an isle appeared ahead; its mountains, as first seen, scarcely to be distinguished from the sky, as they rose out of the blue ocean, now growing more and more distinct, till they assumed new and picturesque forms, some exhibiting dark and rugged rocks, lofty precipices, towering pinnacles, or rounded and gentle slopes covered with umbrageous groves. Here bays or inlets were seen, and green valleys and dark ravines extending far inland. A reef appeared, extending partly round the island, with openings in it through which the ship might sail, and find a secure anchorage within. No dangers appeared ahead; and, skilfully piloted, the Esperanza came to an anchor. Captain Langton, however, like a wise leader, observed carefully how he might speedily again get to sea should circumstances require it. Words would fail to describe the beauty of the island to which the adventurers had come, — the brightness of the atmosphere, the purity of the air, the sparkling waterfalls, the yellow sand, the tall palm-trees, the gorgeous flowers, the groves, the valleys, and the mountains before mentioned. There were natives; for their habitations of considerable size and varied form were perceived amid the trees. Before long, some were seen coming off in canoes; but it seemed that the ship was a strange thing to them, for none of them dared approach her. As observed at a distance, they were dark-skinned men, tall of figure, with much rude ornament, and their hair curiously dressed out in various forms. Still it was possible that they might be mild and gentle of disposition; and as the adventurers were anxious to hold communication with them, Master Weedon offered to visit the shore, and, presenting trinkets and such-like things which had been brought for the purpose, invite them on board.

It was with no small amount of anxiety that he was watched, as, with four men in his boat, he approached the beach. No one drew nearer till he had landed: when, taking the treasures he had brought from the boat, he held them up, first towards one canoe, then towards another; and then he placed them on the sand, and returned to his boat. Thus tempted, the savages landed, and quickly made their way towards the articles on the beach. They were soon seized on and examined; and in a brief space of time afterwards the savages seemed as ready to go on board the ship as they before seemed desirous of keeping away from her. Before long, canoes appeared from many other quarters. Captain Langton, observing this, considered a while, and then called Hugh to him.

"There is a saying, Master Hugh, that we should look upon all men as honest till we find them rogues; but methinks it were safer in these regions to consider all rogues till we find from long experience that they are honest," he observed. "Now, I suspect, from the way these people at first avoided us, they had some reason to believe we would do them harm; but that, seeing that such is not our thought, they now come without fear of us. From this I argue that some other ship has been here, to whose company they gave cause of offence; and they might suppose that our ship is the same, or that we have come to avenge the injury they may have done our friends. We will not say this to the ladies, lest it alarm them without cause; but we will take due precautions against treachery, of which they are assuredly capable, or their looks belie them."

Hugh fully agreed with Captain Langton in his opinion, and Master Weedon and the other officers of the ship were warned to be on their guard. Many of the savages had by this time collected round the ship, and a few chiefs and others came on board. Beatrice and Constance had retired to their cabin; for they neither liked the appearance of the savages, nor desired to be seen of them. They looked curiously at every thing on board, especially at the guns, of the use of which they clearly had some idea. As evening drew on, they took their departure, seemingly on excellent terms with their white visitors. The seamen began to consider them very well-behaved savages; but Captain Langton warned them not to trust to appearances, nor would he allow any of the crew to visit the shore.

The next day, some large canoes came sailing up from other parts of the coast, and many more savages assembled round the ship. Nearly half the ship's company had been below, either asleep or engaged in various occupations, when the savages were on board the first day. Captain Langton, remembering this, determined to keep half the people concealed, and at the same time well armed, while those on deck also were armed; the guns were loaded, the slow matches ready, the cable was hove short, and the sails loosed.

"Maybe the savages mean us well, and these precautions may prove not to have been necessary," he observed to Hugh, who seemed to think that he was over-careful; "but suppose they mean us ill, and purpose suddenly setting on us, we shall have cause to be thankful that we took them. I know what savages are; and I need not tell thee, if they were to succeed, what would be the fate of those you love best, and of all on board. I like not the looks of these gentry; though, for naked savages, their manners are wondrously courteous."

Hugh could not but agree that his friend was

right; though it was tantalizing not to be allowed to wander along that glittering strand, or through those shady groves, or to climb those picturesque hills he gazed at with so much admiration. Water and fuel were, however, to be got off, and, if possible, vegetables: as to meat, as no animals were seen, it was concluded that none was to be obtained. Three or four chiefs and about a dozen followers were allowed on board, and to them was explained by signs what was required. The chiefs quickly understood, and, after talking some time together, ordered away ten of the canoes to the shore; still leaving, however, the same number alongside, full of men armed with clubs and spears. They themselves, however, showed no inclination to quit the ship, but rather to remain to acquaint themselves with every thing about her. They seemed much disconcerted at not being allowed to go below; and for some time sat moodily on the deck, addressing no one. When, however, the canoes were seen coming off, they again rose to their feet, and their animation returned: but, instead of ten, there were now thirty canoes; ten appeared to be laden with calabashes of water, ten with wood chopped fit for burning, and ten with roots and vegetables.

"Surely these people mean us no ill, or they would not thus attend to our wants," cried Hugh, who had from the first been unwilling to mistrust them.

"Wait till we see how they proceed," answered Captain Langton.

The savages now thronged more thickly than ever round the ship. Many sprang on board, and they began to hand up the calabashes and wood; but Hugh observed, on looking down over the side, that there was no large quantity of either wood or water, and that many more people had come on board than were necessary to perform the work. The seamen had rolled some casks up to the side, that the water might be emptied into them; so that, for that purpose, no one need have come on deck. The savages, too, began to mingle among the crew; and Captain Langton observed that three or four attached themselves especially to each seaman, and at the same time that more canoes were coming off from the shore. Matters had already proceeded far enough. Ordering his men to be on their guard, and to separate themselves from the savages, he signified to the chiefs that he was ready to pay them with the articles he had promised, but that their countrymen must leave the ship. The chiefs gazed around: there were at least four savages to one Englishman on board, and ten times as many around the ship. A signal was made, and in an instant each black man raised his club to strike a sailor.

"Hugh, beware!" cried Captain Langton, presenting his pistol at the breast of a chief whose club was about to dash out young Willoughby's brains.

Hugh sprang aside; the savage fell, whirling his club in the air. The seamen, mostly on the watch, avoided the blows of the savages, returning them with interest with their sharp hangers or battle-axes. The report of the captain's pistol was the signal for those below to appear. Up through the hatches they sprang, shooting, cutting down, and driving before them, the treacherous blacks. They quickly fought their way up to the guns, one of which, discharged, made the natives in the canoes paddle off in terror towards the shore. Not so the chiefs. Two seamen lay stretched lifeless on the deck from the blows of their clubs; others were wounded. They themselves stood whirling their heavy weapons around them. A shot laid one low; another, the youngest, driven to the bulwarks, having hurled his club at his foes, sprang overboard, and attempted to reach the canoes by swimming; while a third, fighting to the last, was cut down by Master Weedon's hanger. A few of the canoes were struck by the shots; but the greater number escaped unhurt to the shore.

While the guns were still firing, Beatrice and Constance appeared on deck, and entreated that the savages might be spared. Although Captain Langton and Master Weedon considered such leniency ill bestowed, they obeyed the wishes of the fair ladies they served.

The nature of these savages was, however, before long, proved. Not many hours had passed when warlike sounds of horns and drums, with shrieks and cries, were heard; and round a point were seen coming towards the ship a fleet of large canoes, each like two vessels joined together with one mast and huge sail. Five, ten, nearly twenty, were counted. Nearly a hundred men were on board each; and, by their fierce and frantic gestures, there could be no doubt what were their intentions. It was possible that the guns of the Esperanza might have destroyed many of them, if not the whole: but such a wise commander as Captain Langton considered that nothing would be gained by remaining, and much might be lost; and, as the wind was fair to pass through the nearest passage in the reef, he ordered the anchor to be tripped, the sails to be sheeted home; and, before the canoes got near, the Esperanza, under all sail, was standing out to sea.

"Once on the open ocean, with a fair breeze, I care not how many of those savages come round us," cried the captain, as he guided the ship towards the passage in the reef.

Every man was at his station to trim the sails; for, should the fickle wind change or fall, the Esperanza might be cast helplessly on the rugged mass of coral near which she was passing. The savages showed that they had no intention of abandoning their prey, while stronger proof was given of Captain Langton's wisdom in being cautious of them. The rocks, over which the water formed and leaped, were on every side.

The Esperanza glided on. It seemed that a person might spring from her yard-arms to the rocks. It was here the savages must have hoped to overtake her. They were close astern, and the warriors on their decks even now began to cast their darts towards the ship. Had there been but a few minutes' delay in getting under way, they would have come alongside at a moment most perilous to the safety of the ship. A loud cheer burst from the lips of the British seamen as they found themselves once more on the open ocean. Still their persevering foes came on. By their numbers alone, should they once succeed in getting alongside, they might gain the victory. The after-guns were pointed towards the headmost canoes; but though struck by the shot, and though several of their warriors were killed, they yet came on. So rapidly, too, did they glide over the water, that many of them ranged up on either side. Little could they, however, have expected the shower of shot and bullets which crashed down upon them, tearing open the sides of their frail vessels, rending their sails, shattering the masts, and sweeping the warriors off their decks. It would have been scant mercy to themselves had the adventurers shown mercy. Some of the canoes got alongside; and the enraged savages, attempting to climb up, were driven back with pike and pistol and battle-axe, while the big guns, playing down on them, tore open the sides of their canoes, and sent them to the bottom, leaving those on board to swim for their lives. Soon the whole sea astern of the ship was alive with the forms of the savages as they swam on, either to reach the canoes of their friends or to gain the shore. The breeze increased. The Esperanza rushed through the water. In vain the savages attempted to get on board: numbers had been slain, half their finest canoes had been sunk or disabled. With gratitude and rejoicing the adventurers saw the remainder, suddenly altering their sails, dash towards the shore.

On this one occasion, not an Englishman had been wounded. They waited till they had got far out to sea before they committed to the deep the bodies of their poor shipmates killed in the morning. The breeze which had enabled them to escape from the savages increased rapidly to a gale, and the gale to a fearful storm. They would thankfully have been within the shelter of some friendly port. Dangers seemed thickening around them. On drove the ship; the wild seas reared their foaming heads on either side, the wind howled and whistled through the rigging, the thunder roared, the lightning flashed. Darkness came on; but still the helpless ship drove before the tempest.

Brave Hugh remembered whose son he was, and never lost heart. He went into the cabin, where his sister and Constance were seated, — their hands clasped together, — for the purpose of encouraging them; for the way in which the stout ship rolled and pitched and tumbled about, the timbers and bulkheads groaned and creaked, the water washed overhead, combined with the sounds before described and the shouts of the seamen, made him conclude that they would be overcome with terror.

"Why should we be alarmed?" asked Beatrice, looking up. "We have been protected hitherto: why not to the end? We calculated the risks we were to run before we embarked: we are prepared for all the dangers we may have to encounter."

"Brave sister!" cried Hugh as he left the cabin to return to his duty on deck. "I pray that Edward, for whom you have sacrificed so much, may prove worthy of you, should we succeed in finding him."

All night long the ship drove on before the gale. No object even a cable's length ahead could have been discerned, except when the bright flashes of lightning, darting from the inky clouds, played over the foam-crests of the heavy seas. Who could tell at what moment the good ship might be cast on some coral reef or on some desert shore, and be dashed to fragments? What prospect that the life of any one of them would be saved? or if by any unexpected means their lives should be preserved, that they should escape from falling into the power of savages such as those whom they had lately encountered?

Dawn approached. With daylight, dangers might be seen, and perchance avoided. The spirits of all rose. Those on the watch ahead looked out eagerly for the first faint streaks of light in the eastern sky. Suddenly a cry arose,— a fearful cry to those who knew its import,—

"Land ahead! Breakers ahead!"

"Down with the helm! Haul the starboard tacks aboard, the sheets well aft!" cried Captain Langton in a tone which showed no sign of trepidation. "We may yet weather yonder reef, if the mast proves faithful. Courage, friends; courage!"

Each order was promptly obeyed. The ship heeled over to the blast, staggering through the seas. The reef might be avoided; but there was a point beyond that it seemed impossible to weather. Captain Langton shook his head.

"Heaven may preserve our lives, but the fate of the good ship is sealed," he answered to Hugh's inquiries. "Be prepared to bring your sweet sister and Mistress Raymond on deck. Assure them that each man on board will cheerfully yield up his own life so that theirs may be preserved."

Hugh entered the cabin. In a short time he returned, conducting the two fair girls. They gazed around, not without terror; and yet they retained a calmness and self-possession which many of the other sex might have envied. On one side was the raging sea, on the other a smiling island; but dark rocks, the dread of mariners, intervened.

"Heaven will assuredly hear our prayer, and cause the wild waves to take us, rather than that we should fall into the hands of savages such as those from whom we have just escaped," said Beatrice in answer to a remark of her friend.

"Yet there are savages. Even now I see a numerous band moving along the shore!" exclaimed Constance.

"Still be of courage, sweet sister. The ship may hold together; and we have arms with which to fight, and brave men to use them."

The seamen, though striving to the utmost, knew that the unavoidable catastrophe was approaching. Already the ship was embayed, and the captain was looking out for some spot where she might, with the best chance of preserving their lives, be allowed to drive on shore, should the last resource fail. The anchors had been got ready to let go. Trusty seamen stood with gleaming axes to cut away the masts. Hugh hurried his charges under shelter; for Captain Langton's uplifted hand showed what was about to occur. The shrouds were severed, the axes struck the tall masts, and one by one they fell into the raging sea. One anchor was let go, and speedily another.

"Do the anchors hold?" was the cry.

"Ay, ay," was the answer. "The ship no longer drives; the wind is falling; the sea breaks here with far less force than farther out. Heaven be praised! Even now the ship may be saved!"

Such were the exclamations uttered by those on board the Esperanza. The ship had driven into a bay, where, against all expectation, the anchors held. Should the gale not again increase, fresh masts might be procured from the shore, and the voyage be continued. All depended on the character of the natives. Persons were observed moving on the beach, and apparently watching the ship;

but the sea was yet too rough to allow any boats to come off with safety. Gradually the wind went down, and Captain Langton resolved to communicate with the shore, in order to ascertain the character of the inhabitants, that, at all events, the ladies, and a party to guard them, might be placed in safety till he could get the ship into a secure harbor. The shore was anxiously scanned by all. The natives were still there. One man, who possessed the best eyesight in the ship, affirmed that the savages were white, and wore clothes; though, as might be supposed, his assertion met with the ridicule it deserved.

"We shall soon know the truth," cried Hugh, who, with his sister and Constance, had been the most eager of the spectators; "for here come two canoes, which will speedily be alongside."

"Who can those be? not savages, surely," cried Constance, as the leading canoe drew near.

"My heart tells me, e'en though my eyes might play me false;" exclaimed Beatrice, trembling as she had not with the terror of the expected shipwreck.

In another minute, Edward Raymond had sprung up the side of the Esperanza, and had pressed her in his arms; scarcely heeding, for an instant, his own sweet sister Constance.

"Among faithful, loving, daring women, surpassing all! Now we are rewarded for all our toils and dangers!" he exclaimed, as he looked again and again at the countenance of his beloved Beatrice to assure himself that it was she who rested on one arm, while his other hand pressed that of his devoted sister.

In the second canoe came Antony Waymouth.

Constance received him, as in duty bound, as a relative, albeit a distant one. Whether or not he came up to the picture her imagination had painted of a perfect knight, our chronicle says not. Certain, however, is it, that from the moment his eyes beheld her, and he heard of the sacrifice she had made to friendship in accompanying the fair Beatrice, his heart became enslaved, under the belief that she would be willing to make a far greater sacrifice for love.

Thus had the chief object of the voyage of the Esperanza been accomplished, — the long-lost adventurers were found. Much, however, had still to be done. The boats were lowered, and the ladies, with Hugh Willoughby and a few of the mariners who were sick, were conveyed on shore. The savages, it was found, had made their escape from the island; and, believing that the spirit who protected the white man had come there to punish them for their crime, no more returned to it.

The Esperanza was, the next day, towed into the harbor where lay the battered hull of the Lion. All her company were thankful that they had not repaired her before, and sailed away; and it was unanimously agreed that her rich freight should be transferred to the Esperanza, in which ship all should sail back to Old England. The masts intended for the Lion were placed in the Esperanza, which, in a wonderfully short space of time, was got ready for sea. Certain it is, that, conducted by Master Walker, a service was held, both crews being present, to return thanks for their preservation thus far, and to offer up prayers for their protection for the future. And, moreover, it seemed clear and undoubted, if ladies have to wander round the world, it is advisable, meet, and convenient, if possible, that they should have husbands to protect them: therefore the same excellent minister was called on to unite in the bonds of holy matrimony Master Antony Waymouth and Mistress Constance Raymond, and Master Edward Raymond, the brother of the above Constance, and Mistress Beatrice Willoughby, before the Esperanza once more sailed on her homeward voyage to Old England.

Traversing the vast Pacific towards the east, and rounding the southern point of the New World, the Esperanza reached Plymouth; and never ship returned home with richer freight of gold and of precious stones, or truer or more loving hearts. And here, in the peaceful haven, endeth our "Chronicle of the Sea."

THE END.

J. E. TILTON & CO.'S PUBLICATIONS.

JUVENILE BOOKS.

THE Drummer Boy

BY THE AUTHOR OF

"*FATHER BRIGHTHOPES.*"

A splendid Story, for Boys, of Camp Life and War Scenes. Handsomely illustrated by F. O. C. DARLEY.

IT DON'T NEED PUSHING.—*Zion's Herald* thus speaks of The Drummer Boy: "Among the boys, this is the most popular and interesting book of the season. They not only read it through, but advertise it, and make the other boys uneasy until they read it. In some instances, school-teachers have it read aloud to all the school. It will sell without pushing."

Price $1.50

J. E. TILTON & CO.'S PUBLICATIONS.

DICK ONSLOW'S ADVENTURES AMONG THE REDSKINS. By W. G. H. KINGSTON.

"This is an illustrated story of adventures, of hair-breadth escapes among the Indians, wild beasts, &c. *The boys' delight.*"— *Exchange.*

Price $1.50

ANTONY WAYMOUTH; or, THE GENTLEMEN ADVENTURERS. By KINGSTON, author of "Dick Onslow among the Redskins." *Nearly ready.*

Price $1.50

THE LIFE-BOAT. By R. M. BALLANTYNE. Published in England and America simultaneously.

"Sea-loving boys will heartily enjoy 'The Life-Boat, a Tale of our Coast Heroes,' wherein Mr. R. M. Ballantyne describes the brave deeds of the rude fishermen who peril their lives to rescue their fellow-creatures from wrecked vessels. Mr. Ballantyne's name on the title-page of a schoolboy's book has for some years been a guaranty to buyers that the volume is cheap at its price; but he has not written a better story than the present. A spirited artist has aided him effectually; and the historic chapter on life-boats is a good feature of the work."— *London Athenæum.*

Price $1.50

THE BOBBIN BOY. A Life of MAJOR-GENERAL N. P. BANKS. Illustrated by BILLINGS.

Price $1.50

THE PRINTER BOY. A Life of BENJAMIN FRANKLIN. Illustrated by HAMMATT BILLINGS.

Price $1.50

J. E. TILTON & CO.'S PUBLICATIONS.

FAIRY DREAMS.

A BEAUTIFUL ILLUSTRATED FAIRY BOOK.

"Gentle stories from the rare and wonderful Fairy-land, told in exquisite language. Printed on delicately tinted paper, and illustrated with fine engravings." — *Daily Sentinel.*

Price $1.00

ABEL GRAY. A beautifully illustrated little volume, reprinted from the London Religious Tract Society's edition.

Price . . . . 50 cents.

J. E. TILTON & CO.'S PUBLICATIONS.

THE PLYMOUTH-ROCK SERIES.

The three following volumes are now ready: —

The Little Rebel.
The Tailor Boy.
Willard Prime.

Each volume in this series is written by one of the best modern writers for the young, unconnected, beautifully illustrated and bound. It is intended by the publishers that it shall far excel all former libraries of similar character. The manner in which they are named by the public is highly encouraging to the publishers.

"We have had occasion before to notice the 'Plymouth-Rock Stories,' published, in their usual admirable manner, by J. E. Tilton & Co. Every juvenile book which inculcates high morality, true honor, and religious feeling, is a gain to the world. Boys and girls *will* read; and it is important that the books they have should be those calculated to mould their characters on the highest plane. We believe this to be the aim of this series; and we therefore give it a cordial welcome, and bespeak for it the interest of the community." — *Christian Register.*

Price, each $1.00
Sold separately, or the three in a neat box.

THE ALDEN JUVENILES.

The Light-Hearted Girl.
The Lost Lamb.
The Cardinal Flower.
The Burial of the First-Born.

The above four are by REV. JOSEPH ALDEN, D.D. They are furnished in a neat box, and beautifully illustrated.

"These four compose a series of most beautiful and fascinating storybooks for children." — *Syracuse Daily Courier.*

"Dr. Alden has long been a favorite writer of books for the young; and all his books have the excellent quality of being good in their moral influence." — *Boston Recorder.*

Price, each . . . . . 50 cents.

J. E. TILTON & CO.'S PUBLICATIONS.

THE LIFE AND ADVENTURES OF

DANDY JACK.

Full of Pictures of Animals.

"An ingeniously told story of a monkey, which not only, from beginning to end, amuses the youthful reader, but teaches him lessons of natural history."

Price . . . . 75 cents.

FRANKIE'S BOOK OF BIBLE MEN.

SUSAN AND FRANKIE.

SABBATH TALKS ABOUT JESUS.

SABBATH TALKS ON THE PSALMS OF DAVID.

"It is enough to say that these little volumes are written by Mrs. S. G. Ashton, and published by Messrs. J. E. Tilton & Co., to insure their hearty welcome, and a guaranty that they are as attractive as possible in interest to the reader, and beauty of illustrations and binding." — *Enquirer.*

Price, each . . . . . 50 cents.

J. E. TILTON & CO.'S PUBLICATIONS.

THE WINNIE AND WALTER STORIES.

The Story of Our Darling Nellie.

Story-Telling at Thanksgiving.

Christmas Stories.

Talks about Old Times.

The above four are by the same author, elegantly illustrated, and furnished in a neat box.

"Somebody is writing a series of agreeable stories, for children, about Winnie and Walter. The writer has evidently once been young, and has not forgotten the time. Nay, we should also judge that he has seen and conversed with children at a recent date, and possibly has some juvenile relatives who have aided in an important part of his education; for it is quite true that children are efficient educators, and, altogether, furnish a discipline which few can afford to do without. In return for this service, we too often give them a literature unsuited to their tastes, if not beyond their comprehension. But these books present no picture of tiny saints upon stilts, or of patient martyrs to incessant moral lectures. Theirs is a healthy, genuine, unmitigated childhood, of which a true manhood is the ripened and appropriate fruit." — *Springfield Republican.*

Price, each . . . . . . 50 cents.

PACK OF REWARDS. Containing THE TEN COMMANDMENTS; THE LORD'S PRAYER; SELECTIONS FROM THE SERMON ON THE MOUNT, AND THE PSALMS. (16 cards in all.) Beautifully illustrated.

Net, 75 cents per dozen packs; $5.00 per hundred packs.

www.ingramcontent.com/pod-product-compliance
Lightning Source LLC
Chambersburg PA
CBHW030745230426
43667CB00007B/843